STUDENT ACTIVITIES MANUAL

to Accompany

¡Trato hecho!
Spanish for Real Life

Third Edition

John T. McMinn
Austin Community College

Nuria Alonso García
Providence College

PEARSON
Prentice
Hall

Upper Saddle River, New Jersey 07458

Executive Editor: *Bob Hemmer*
Executive Director of Market Development: *Kristine Suárez*
Senior Development Editor: *Julia Caballero*
Production Supervision: *Nancy Stevenson*
Full-Service/Project Management: *Natalie Hansen and Sue Katkus, Schawk, Inc.*
Assistant Director of Production: *Mary Rottino*
Assistant Editor: *Meriel Martínez Moctezuma*
Media Editor: *Samantha Alducin*
Media Production Manager: *Roberto Fernandez*
Prepress and Manufacturing Buyer: *Christina Helder*
Interior and Cover Design: *Van Mua, Schawk, Inc.*
Senior Marketing Manager: *Jacquelyn Zautner*
Electronic Page Layout: *Schawk, Inc.*
Publisher: *Phil Miller*

This book was set in 10.5/12.5 Minion and was printed
and bound by Bradford & Bigelow. The cover and endpapers
were printed by Bradford & Bigelow.

Printed in the United States of America
10 9 8 7 6 5 4 3

ISBN: 0-13-191410-3

Prentice-Hall International (UK) Limited, London
Prentice-Hall of Australia Pty. Limited, Sydney
Prentice-Hall Canada Inc., Toronto
Prentice-Hall Hispanoamericana, S.A., Mexico
Prentice-Hall of India Private Limited, New Delhi
Prentice-Hall of Japan, Inc., Tokyo
Pearson Education Asia Pte. Ltd., Singapore
Editora Prentice-Hall do Brasil, Ltda., Rio de Janeiro

CONTENTS

Note to the Student

This **Student Activities Manual** was created to accompany **¡Trato hecho! Third Edition.**

The Manual activities are designed to help you further develop your reading and writing skills while practicing the vocabulary and grammar points featured in your textbook. Each lesson in the Manual corresponds to the topics presented in your textbook.

The purpose of the Manual is to serve as a rewarding experience that will enhance your proficiency in Spanish. Take full advantage of all that the Manual segments have to offer. When you have completed the Manual activities, take the time to work on your pronunciation to improve your oral proficiency in Spanish. Each of the activities blends grammar and vocabulary topics from the textbook to provide optimum learning to you, the student. The Manual segments were designed, in part, based on comments from students and instructors who have enjoyed using the text from its first edition. If you feel that the speakers on the audio go too fast, you are not alone. There are several ways that you can improve your understanding.

- Listen to the audio a while longer to pinpoint the trouble spots and to pick up the gist of the exercise.
- After you have determined the trouble spots, listen to the audio again, with your textbook open to the corresponding pages.
- If needed, ask your professor to show you the Audioscript.

Although this method might take a little extra time, your efforts will start to pay off quickly. By listening to the audio and repeating what you hear, you will gain valuable skills in speaking Spanish. Since the activities of each **Tema** of the Manual carefully match the content of the corresponding **Tema** in the textbook, you are very likely to fill in any comprehension gaps.

¡Bienvenidos!

1 ¡A conocernos!

Tema 1 ¿Cómo te llamas? ¿Cómo estás?

1-1 ¿Cómo estás? Would they more likely use the following expressions in scene **A** or scene **B**? Write each one under the corresponding illustration.

Buenos días.	¿Cómo estás?	Estoy muy bien.
Buenas tardes.	¿Cómo está?	Estoy mal.

A

_____

_____

_____

B

_____

_____

_____

1-2 Un nuevo estudiante. You and Ramiro, a new student from Monterrey, Mexico, meet for the first time before class. Complete the following conversation that you have with him.

— (1) _____ días, ¿(2) _____ te llamas?

— (3) _____ Ramiro Villegas.

— ¿Villegas? ¿(4) _____ con v (5) _____ con b?

— Se escribe (6) _____ v. (7) _____ tú, ¿cómo

　　(8) _____?

— Me llamo (9) _____.

— (10) _____ gusto.

— (11) _____.

1-3 ¿Formal o familiar? Rewrite the following questions changing them from the formal (**usted**) form to the familiar (**tú**) form.

1. ¿Cómo se llama Ud.? _____

2. ¿Cómo está Ud.? _____

3. ¿De dónde es Ud.? _____

1-4 ¿Y tú? There are two verbs meaning *to be* in Spanish, **ser** and **estar**, so there are two ways to say *I am* or *you are*. Remember to use the forms of **ser (yo soy, tú eres, Ud. es)** to say who people are, where they are from, or what they are like. Use the forms of **estar (yo estoy, tú estás, Ud. está)** to say how people are doing. Complete the following conversation with **ser** or **estar** using the forms for **tú** and **yo**.

— Buenos días, ¿cómo (1) _____?

— (2) _____ muy bien, gracias. Me llamo Anita Méndez. Y tú, ¿cómo te llamas?

— Mucho gusto, Anita. (3) _____ Felicia Fernós.

— ¿De dónde (4) _____, Felicia?

— (5) _____ de Guatemala. ¿Y tú?

— Yo (6) _____ de aquí.

1-5 ¿Y Ud.? Rewrite the preceding conversation with formal forms so that it is between two businesspersons, Federico Alfonso, from Buenos Aires, and Cecilia Núñez, from Montevideo.

_____

_____

_____

_____

_____

_____

_____

_____

1-6 ¿Cómo se escribe? A Hispanic friend is confused about the spelling of the following italicized English words that look like the boldfaced Spanish words. Tell him how they are spelled in English (**en inglés**) by completing the following sentences in Spanish, as in the model.

MODELO   *constitution* – **constitución:**

En inglés, *constitution* **se escribe** sin acento en la (*the*) *o* y **con** *t* en vez de (*instead of*) *c*.

1. *photo* – **foto:** En _____, *photo* _____ con *ph* en vez de *f*.

2. *biology* – **biología:** En inglés, *biology* se escribe _____ *y* en vez de *ía*.

3. *institution* – **institución:** En inglés, *institution* se escribe con _____ en vez de

   _____ y _____ acento en la *o*.

4. *romantic* – **romántico:** En inglés, *romantic* _____ sin

   _____ en la *a* y _____ la *o* final.

5. *independent* – **independiente:** _____

   _____

1-7 Diario. Write a conversation in which a student, Marta Calderón, from Tegucigalpa, Honduras, is meeting you for the first time. In the conversation, you...

- ask how each other is doing.
- find out each other's name.
- ask where each other is from.
- ask Marta how to write Tegucigalpa.

_____

_____

_____

_____

_____

_____

_____

_____

_____

¡A escuchar!

1-8 Saludos. You will hear several greetings or questions. Select the logical response to each one.

1. a. Buenos días.
   b. Hola.
   c. Buenas noches.

2. a. Me llamo Juan.
   b. Estoy bien, gracias.
   c. Buenas tardes.

3. a. Soy Antonio.
   b. ¿Y tú?
   c. Soy de aquí.

4. a. Me llamo Gabriela.
   b. Regular.
   c. Mucho gusto.

5. a. Estoy bien.
   b. Soy Antonio.
   c. Soy de Miami.

1-9 ¿Cómo se escribe? Listen and repeat the alphabet in Spanish.

a a	h hache	ñ eñe	t te
b be (grande)	i i	o o	u u
c ce	j jota	p pe	v uve, ve (chica), ve (corta)
d de	k ka	q cu	w uve doble, doble ve, doble u
e e	l ele	r ere	x equis
f efe	m eme	rr erre	y i griega
g ge	n ene	s ese	z zeta

1-10 Adjetivos. Write each adjective you hear spelled out. You should understand the meaning of these words describing personality traits, because they are similar to adjectives in English.

1. Soy   No soy   _____.

2. Soy   No soy   _____.

3. Soy   No soy   _____.

4. Soy   No soy   _____.

5. Soy   No soy   _____.

Now go back and indicate whether the adjective describes you by selecting **soy** or **no soy**.

1-11 A lo personal. Imagine that a classmate is asking you the questions that you hear. Answer each one with a complete sentence in Spanish.

1. _____

2. _____

3. _____

4. _____

Tema 2 Quiero presentarte a... / Quiero presentarle a...

1-12 Presentaciones. What would you say if you were introducing your friends and family members to the indicated people? Would you use **Quiero presentarte a...** *(familiar)* or **Quiero presentarle a...** *(formal)*?

MODELO *your best friend to an elderly neighbor*
Quiero presentar**le** a **mi mejor amigo.**

1. *your mother to your best friend*

   Quiero presentar_____ a _____.

2. *your father to the dean*

   Quiero presentar_____ a _____.

3. *your (female) classmate to your boyfriend, girlfriend, or spouse*

   Quiero presentar_____ a _____.

4. *your sister to your Spanish instructor*

   Quiero presentar_____ a _____.

1-13 Comparaciones. Compare the following people by filling in the blanks with **más... que, menos... que,** or **tan... como**.

1. Los republicanos son _____ liberales _____ los demócratas.

2. Lance Armstrong es _____ atlético _____ Jennifer López.

3. Ted Koppel es _____ intelectual _____ Peter Jennings.

4. Brad Pitt es _____ romántico _____ David Spade.

5. Ellen DeGeneres es _____ seria _____ Hillary Clinton.

6. Jay Leno es _____ cómico _____ Ted Koppel.

1-14 Caracteres opuestos. Mónica is the opposite of her brother Enrique. Complete the sentences describing them, as in the model.

MODELO Enrique es muy tímido. Mónica no es **tímida**. Es **extrovertida**.

1. Mónica es muy extrovertida. Enrique no es _____. Es _____.

2. Mónica es muy cómica. Enrique no es _____. Es _____.

3. Enrique es muy pesimista. Mónica no es _____. Es _____.

Capítulo 1 • ¡A conocernos! **5**

1-15 ¿Cómo son? A friend says that one adjective from each pair describes the following people and the other one does not. Write each adjective in the appropriate blank, changing its ending as necessary.

MODELO   Mi novia es **extrovertida**. No es muy **seria**.

(serio, extrovertido)

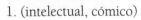

1. (intelectual, cómico)   2. (responsable/impulsivo)   3. (ambicioso, pesimista)

1. Mi padre es _____. No es muy _____.

2. Mi hermana es _____. No es muy _____.

3. Mi hermano es _____. No es muy _____.

4. (atlético, emocional)   5. (religioso, egoísta)   6. (tímido, liberal)

4. Mi mejor amigo es _____. No es muy _____.

5. Mis padres son _____. No son muy _____.

6. Mis amigos son _____. No son muy _____.

1-16 ¿Y tú? Imagine that a classmate runs into you outside of class and asks you the following questions. Complete each question with the correct form of **ser** and answer it with a complete sentence in Spanish.

1. Tú y yo _____ compañeros de clase, ¿no?

   _____

2. ¿Cómo _____ tus profesores este (*this*) semestre/trimestre?

   _____

3. ¿De dónde _____ (tú)?

   _____

4. ¿De dónde _____ tus padres?

   _____

5. ¿Tu mejor amigo/a _____ estudiante (*a student*)?

   _____

6. ¿_____ (tú) más extrovertido/a que tu mejor amigo/a?

   _____

7. ¿_____ ustedes muy serios/as?

   _____

1-17 Diario. Write a self-introduction in which you give the following information:

- your name
- where you are from
- what you are like and what you are not like, describing your personality
- whether you have a boyfriend/girlfriend, where he/she is from, and what he/she is like
- who your best friend is and what he/she is like compared to you

_____

_____

_____

_____

_____

_____

¡A escuchar!

1-18 ¿De quién habla? A friend is talking about her boyfriend (**su novio**) and her best friend, who is a female (**su amiga**). Listen to each statement and indicate who is being described. If you cannot tell, select **c. ???**.

MODELO   You hear: Es muy divertida.
a. su novio   ⓑ su amiga   c. ???

1. a. su novio   b. su amiga   c. ???   4. a. su novio   b. su amiga   c. ???
2. a. su novio   b. su amiga   c. ???   5. a. su novio   b. su amiga   c. ???
3. a. su novio   b. su amiga   c. ???   6. a. su novio   b. su amiga   c. ???

1-19 Comparaciones. Listen to some comparisons of Gabriela and Alicia, who are shown below. Select **a. cierto** if the statement you hear is true according to the illustrations and leave the blank empty. If it is false, select **b. falso**, stop the recording, and write a sentence correcting it in the blank.

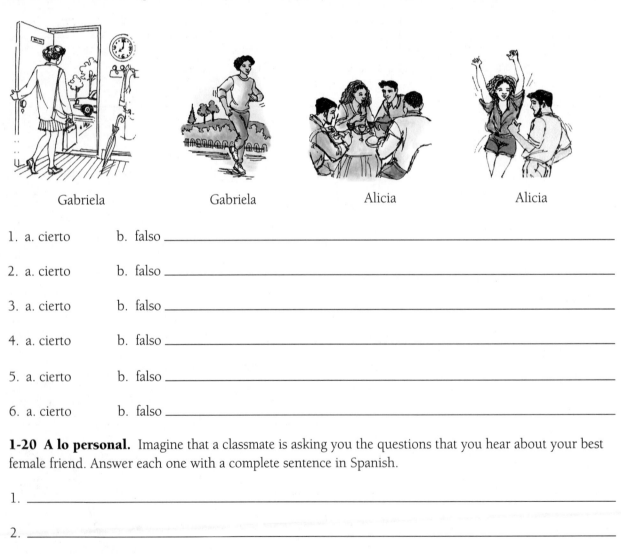

Gabriela   Gabriela   Alicia   Alicia

1. a. cierto   b. falso _____

2. a. cierto   b. falso _____

3. a. cierto   b. falso _____

4. a. cierto   b. falso _____

5. a. cierto   b. falso _____

6. a. cierto   b. falso _____

1-20 A lo personal. Imagine that a classmate is asking you the questions that you hear about your best female friend. Answer each one with a complete sentence in Spanish.

1. _____

2. _____

3. _____

4. _____

Tema 3 ¿Cómo es la universidad? ¿Qué clases tienes?

1-21 ¿En qué universidad? Pick the logical adjective from the list that goes in each blank and complete the sentences. Pay attention to both the meanings and the forms of the adjectives.

| bonita | feas | pequeñas | pequeño | viejos | modernos |

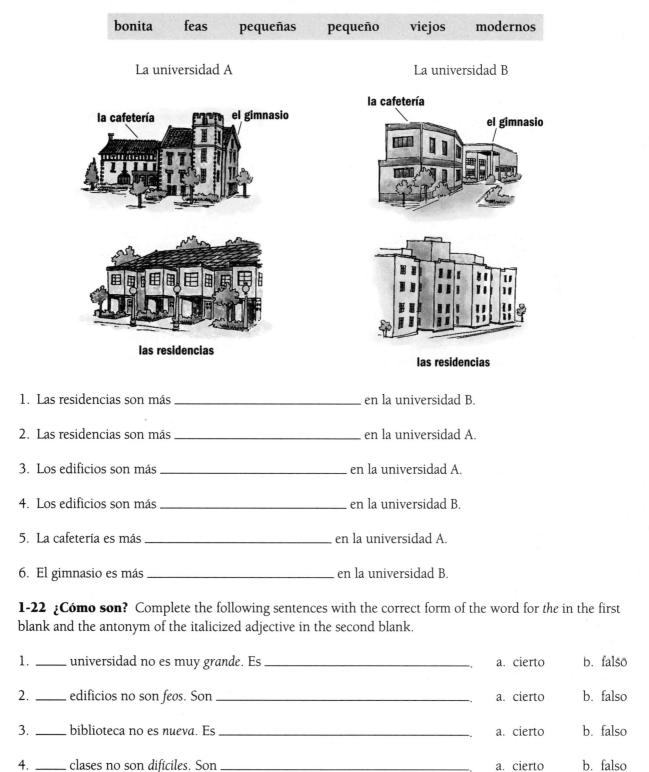

La universidad A   La universidad B

1. Las residencias son más _____ en la universidad B.

2. Las residencias son más _____ en la universidad A.

3. Los edificios son más _____ en la universidad A.

4. Los edificios son más _____ en la universidad B.

5. La cafetería es más _____ en la universidad A.

6. El gimnasio es más _____ en la universidad B.

1-22 ¿Cómo son? Complete the following sentences with the correct form of the word for *the* in the first blank and the antonym of the italicized adjective in the second blank.

1. _____ universidad no es muy *grande*. Es _____.   a. cierto   b. falso

2. _____ edificios no son *feos*. Son _____.   a. cierto   b. falso

3. _____ biblioteca no es *nueva*. Es _____.   a. cierto   b. falso

4. _____ clases no son *difíciles*. Son _____.   a. cierto   b. falso

5. _____ química no es *aburrida*. Es _____.   a. cierto   b. falso

6. _____ profesores no son *perezosos*. Son _____.   a. cierto   b. falso

7. _____ estudiantes no son *antipáticos*. Son _____.   a. cierto   b. falso

8. _____ clase de español no es *grande*. Es _____.   a. cierto   b. falso

9. _____ residencias no son *modernas*. Son _____.   a. cierto   b. falso

Now select **a. cierto** or **b. falso** to indicate whether each statement is true or false for your university.

1-23 Disciplinas. Explain which class does not go with the others (**las otras**) by completing the sentences that follow, as in the model.

MODELO   la biología, la física, la literatura
               Es **la literatura** porque *(because)* las otras clases son **ciencias**.

1. el español, la música, el inglés

   Es _____ porque las otras clases son _____.

2. la informática, la historia, las ciencias políticas

   Es _____ porque las otras clases son _____.

3. las matemáticas, la informática, el francés

   Es _____ porque las otras clases son _____.

4. la contabilidad, el arte, la música

   Es _____ porque las otras clases son _____.

1-24 Mis clases. Write sentences saying whether you have the following classes this semester/trimester. If you do have a class, say what it is like.

MODELO   **Sí, tengo economía este semestre/trimestre. Es interesante, pero es un poco difícil.**
               No, no tengo economía este semestre/trimestre.

1. _____

2. _____

3. _____

4. _____

5. _____

1-25 Preguntas. Imagine that another student asks you the following questions. Answer each one with a complete sentence.

1. ¿Qué clases tienes este semestre?

   _____

2. ¿Cómo son tus clases?

   _____

3. ¿Qué clase es la más difícil?

   _____

4. ¿Qué clase es la más fácil?

   _____

5. ¿Cómo se llama tu profesor/a de español?

   _____

1-26 Diario. Write two paragraphs describing your university and your classes this semester/trimester. Include the following information.

- A description of the buildings, the library, the residence halls, and the cafeteria. (If you need to say there isn't something, use **No hay...** *There isn't / There aren't...*)

- A list of the courses you are taking, whether they are easy and/or interesting, and what your professors and classmates are like.

_____

_____

_____

_____

_____

_____

¡A escuchar!

1-27 ¿En qué clase? Does each sentence you hear describe Professor Durán's class or Professor Orozco's class? Select **a** or **b**.

a. la clase de la profesora Durán

b. la clase del profesor Orozco

1. a b   3. a b   5. a b   7. a b

2. a b   4. a b   6. a b   8. a b

1-28 Una actitud negativa. Pablo always makes negative statements about everything. Answer each question you hear about the university as he would, using the antonym of the adjective you hear. You will then hear the correct answer. Listen and repeat it.

MODELO   You hear: ¿Son bonitos los edificios?
           You answer: **No, los edificios son feos.**
           You hear: No, los edificios son feos.
           You repeat: **No, los edificios son feos.**

1-29 ¿Compañeros de clase? Listen to a conversation in which two classmates talk about their classes and complete the following sentences with the correct information.

1. Él se llama _____ y ella se llama _____.

2. Él es de _____ y ella es de _____.

3. Este semestre él tiene clases de _____

   y ella tiene clases de _____.

4. La clase favorita de él es _____. Es _____ pero el

   profesor es _____. La clase favorita de ella es _____

   porque (*because*) la profesora es _____.

Tema 4 ¿Te gustan las clases? ¿Cuántos estudiantes hay?

1-30 Los hispanos. Spell out the following numbers in the blanks.

a. 11 _____ millones

b. 2.7 _____ punto _____ millones

c. 6.7 _____ punto _____ millones

d. 2.9 _____ punto _____ millones

e. 39 _____ millones

f. el 13 _____ por ciento (%)

g. el 67 _____ por ciento

h. el 9 _____ por ciento

i. el 4 _____ por ciento

j. el 34 _____ por ciento

k. el 43 _____ por ciento

Now guess which number goes with each description of Hispanics in the United States below and write its letter in the blank.

1. _____: el número de hispanos en los Estados Unidos

2. _____: el porcentaje de hispanos en los Estados Unidos de ascendencia mexicana (*Mexican heritage*)

3. _____: el porcentaje de hispanos en los Estados Unidos de ascendencia cubana

4. _____: el porcentaje de hispanos en los Estados Unidos de ascendencia puertorriqueña

5. _____: el número de hispanos en California

6. _____: el número de hispanos en Texas

7. _____: el número de hispanos en Florida

8. _____: el número de hispanos en Nueva York

9. _____: el porcentaje total de la población de los Estados Unidos que (*that*) representan los hispanos

10. _____: el porcentaje total de la población de California o de Texas que representan los hispanos

11. _____: el porcentaje total de la población que representan los hispanos en Nueva México, el estado con mayor (*the greatest*) porcentaje de hispanos

1-31 ¿Cuál es tu número de teléfono? Write out the following telephone numbers as they would be said by a telephone operator.

MODELO   223-4709
          Es el **dos, veintitrés, cuarenta y siete, cero nueve.**

1. 759-1333: Es el _____.

2. 990-3141: Es el _____.

3. 707-1991: Es el _____.

4. 635-2409: Es el _____.

5. 838-9770: Es el _____.

6. 454-6026: Es el _____.

1-32 ¿Le gusta(n)? Alicia is very outgoing and is always with her friends, but she is not very studious. Does she probably like the following things? Complete the following sentences with **le gusta(n)** or **no le gusta(n).** Use the form with **(n)** if what is (not) liked is plural.

1. _____ la tarea.

2. _____ las clases sin mucha tarea.

3. _____ las actividades sociales.

4. _____ los exámenes.

5. _____ estudiar sola.

6. _____ estar con sus amigos.

1-33 Comparaciones. Gabriela always says that her friends and her university are the best and her sister's are really bad. Indicate whether she is talking about herself or her sister in the following sentences by writing the correct form of **mi(s)** *my* or **su(s)** *her* in the blanks.

MODELO   **Mi** novio es muy romántico.

1. _____ novio es antipático.

2. _____ amigos son simpáticos.

3. _____ amigos son divertidos.

4. _____ mejor amiga es egoísta.

5. _____ mejor amiga es muy paciente.

6. _____ profesores son muy interesantes.

7. _____ profesores son aburridos.

8. _____ hermana no es muy inteligente.

1-34 Preguntas. Answer the following questions another student might ask you with complete sentences in Spanish.

1. ¿Cuántas clases tienes este semestre?

    _____

2. ¿Cuál (*Which*) es la clase más grande? ¿Cuántos estudiantes hay?

    _____

3. ¿Cuál es la clase más pequeña? ¿Cuántos estudiantes hay?

    _____

4. ¿En qué clase tienes más tarea?

    _____

5. ¿Cuántos exámenes hay en la clase de español este semestre?

    _____

6. ¿Qué clase(s) te gusta(n)? ¿Qué clase(s) no te gusta(n)?

    _____

1-35 Diario. Write a paragraph describing your classes this semester. Tell how many students there are more or less (**más o menos**) in each one, what the class, professor, and students are like, whether there is a lot of homework, and how many tests there are this semester.

_____

_____

_____

_____

_____

_____

_____

_____

¡A escuchar!

1-36 Códigos secretos. You will hear some questions a friend has put into secret code as a series of numbers. As you hear each number, use the chart to decipher the letters and write them in the blanks. After completing both questions, answer each one with a complete sentence.

MODELO   You hear: 2, 9, 28, 5, 22, 2, 21, 9, 22, 2, 5, 6, 1, 21, 15, 19, 1, 2, 9, 15, 21, 2, 5, 15, 21
    You write: ¿<u>T</u> <u>e</u> <u>g</u> <u>u</u> <u>s</u> <u>t</u> <u>a</u> <u>e</u> <u>s</u> <u>t</u> <u>u</u> <u>d</u> <u>i</u> <u>a</u> <u>r</u> <u>l</u> <u>i</u> <u>t</u> <u>e</u> <u>r</u> <u>a</u> <u>t</u> <u>u</u> <u>r</u> <u>a</u>?
    You answer: **Sí, me gusta estudiar literatura. / No, no me gusta estudiar literatura.**

1 i	5 u	9 e	13 b	17 o	21 a	25 y
2 t	6 d	10 rr	14 k	18 m	22 s	26 q
3 j	7 n	11 c	15 r	19 l	23 w	27 p
4 ñ	8 x	12 z	16 f	20 v	24 h	28 g

1. ¿__ __ __ __ __ __ __ __ __ __ __ __ __ __ __ __ __ __?

   _____

2. ¿__ __ __ __ __ __ __ __ __ __ __ __ __ __ __ __ __ __ __ __ __ __ __ __?

   _____

1-37 Matemáticas. Give the correct answer to each math problem you hear. Then listen as each problem is repeated with the answer and write it out using numerals.

MODELO   You hear: ¿Cuánto son seis más siete?
    You answer: **Seis más siete son trece.**
    You hear: Seis más siete son trece.
    You write: **6 + 7 = 13**

1. _____ + _____ = _____

2. _____ + _____ = _____

3. _____ + _____ = _____

4. _____ + _____ = _____

5. _____ + _____ = _____

6. _____ + _____ = _____

1-38 ¿Qué tal las clases? Listen to a conversation in which a student talks to a friend about her classes. Then answer the following questions about her with complete sentences.

1. ¿Qué clase no le gusta mucho? ¿Por qué?

   _____

2. ¿Qué clases le gustan? ¿Por qué?

   _____

3. ¿Cuántos estudiantes hay en sus clases?

   _____

Tema 5 ¿Qué hora es? ¿Cuándo son tus clases?

1-39 ¿Qué hora es? Write sentences saying what time it is on each clock.

1.   2.   3.    4.   5.

1. _____

2. _____

3. _____

4. _____

5. _____

1-40 ¡Estás confundido! You have a friend who is always a day off. Tell him that everything is the day before.

MODELO   Trabajo el sábado, ¿verdad? (*right?*)
           No, trabajas el viernes.

1. Mañana es domingo, ¿verdad?

_____

2. Esta (*This*) tarea es para el viernes, ¿verdad?

_____

3. Quieres estudiar para el examen el martes, ¿verdad?

_____

4. El examen es el miércoles, ¿verdad?

_____

1-41 ¿Dónde está Ramón? Complete the following sentences saying in which place the man from the following illustrations probably is at the indicated times. Write out the time as in the model.

en casa   en el autobús   en el trabajo

MODELO   8:15 a.m.: **A las ocho y quince de la mañana** está **en casa**.

1. 8:45 a.m.: _____ está _____.

2. 9:00 a.m.: _____ está _____.

3. 10:15 a.m.: _____ está _____.

4. 12:00 p.m.: _____ está _____.

5. 3:30 p.m.: _____ está _____.

6. 6:50 p.m.: _____ está _____.

1-42 Los días de clase. Complete the following description of a student's class day by writing the correct words in the blanks.

Generalmente (1) _____ (el, los) lunes, miércoles y viernes estoy (2) _____ (en, a) casa

(3) _____ (de, por) la mañana y tengo dos clases (4) _____ (de, por) la tarde. Una

clase es (5) _____ (a la, a las) una de la tarde (6) _____ (y, e) la otra clase es

(7) _____ (a la, a las) tres. Son clases de literatura (8) _____ (y, e) historia.

(9) _____ (El, Los) lunes y miércoles trabajo (10) _____ (de, a) cinco a nueve, pero

(11) _____ (el, los) viernes no trabajo. Esta semana (12) _____ (es, hay) un examen

(13) _____ (el, los) miércoles y necesito (*I need*) estudiar todo el día (14) _____

(el, los) martes.

1-43 Preguntas. Answer the following questions another student might ask you with complete sentences in Spanish.

1. ¿Qué día es hoy?

   _____

2. ¿Te gusta más estudiar por la mañana, por la tarde o por la noche?

   _____

3. ¿Tienes más clases por la mañana, por la tarde o por la noche?

   _____

4. ¿Qué días y a qué hora es la clase de español?

   _____

5. ¿Qué días y a qué hora trabajas?

   _____

1-44 Diario. Write a paragraph saying when you like to have **(tener)** classes. Then say whether you like your schedule this semester/trimester **(este semestre/trimestre)**, giving the days and times of each class. Finally, say whether you work, and if so, what days and at what times.

_____

_____

_____

_____

_____

_____

_____

_____

_____

_____

¡A escuchar!

1-45 Los acentos gráficos. Words that end with a vowel or the consonants **s** or **n** have a written accent mark on the stressed vowel if it is not in the *next-to-last* syllable. As you hear the following words pronounced, write an accent mark on the stressed vowel if one is needed.

1. ran-cho
2. au-to-ma-ti-co
3. te-le-fo-no

4. ne-ga-ti-vo
5. ex-ce-len-te
6. hi-po-cri-ta

7. va-lien-te
8. mier-co-les
9. do-min-go

10. sa-ba-do
11. pre-o-cu-pa-do
12. es-tas

Words ending with consonants other than **s** or **n** have a written accent mark on the stressed vowel if it is not in the *last* syllable. As you hear the following words pronounced, write an accent mark on the stressed vowel if one is needed.

1. fe-no-me-nal
2. o-por-tu-ni-dad

3. di-fi-cil
4. es-tu-diar

5. pro-fe-sor
6. u-til

7. Mar-ti-nez
8. Go-mez

1-46 Mi horario. Listen as a student talks about his schedule to a friend. Write the name of each of his classes on the following weekly planner, indicating the days and times. Also write **trabajo** indicating the days and times he works.

HORARIO	LUNES	MARTES	MIÉRCOLES	JUEVES	VIERNES	SÁBADO	DOMINGO
9-10:00							
10-11:00							
11-12:00							
12-1:00							
1-2:00							
2-3:00							
3-4:00							
4-5:00							
5-6:00							
6-7:00							

¡Trato hecho!

1-47 En la red. In this section of each chapter of the workbook, you will be asked to search the Web for information about Hispanic culture and the Spanish language. There will be suggestions of what to look for, but you are encouraged to extend your search to other related topics. In this chapter you will be searching for statistics and projections concerning the Hispanics in the United States. Begin by searching for *U.S. Census Bureau Hispanics*. Check the sites you find for the information requested below and answer the questions in English. Write down the addresses of the interesting and useful sites you discover and share them with your instructor and other students.

Addresses of useful and interesting sites:

www._____

www._____

www._____

1. What is the current number of Hispanics living in the United States and what percent of the total population do they represent? How are those numbers projected to change in the future?

   _____

   _____

   _____

   _____

2. What information can you find on family structure or home life among Hispanics living in the United States?

   _____

   _____

   _____

3. What information can you find on the education and employment of Hispanics in the United States?

   _____

   _____

   _____

1-48 Composición. Using what you have written in each *Diario* section for this chapter, write a letter to a new Hispanic penpal explaining who you are and telling about your life at the university.

You may begin the letter with **Querido/a...** *(Dear...)* and a name of your choice.

In the first paragraph, give your name, where you are from, and what you are like. Also say how many brothers and sisters you have, what they and your parents are like, and compare your personality to other family members, using some adjectives from p. 8 of the textbook.

In the second paragraph, describe your schedule, stating the classes you have this semester, when they are, whether you like them, and why. Also mention how many students there are in each one and describe your professors and classmates as well.

In the third paragraph, describe places around campus, and tell what you like or do not like about the university.

Finally, close by asking your penpal two or three questions about himself/herself, and end with **Un saludo...** *(Regards, Best wishes from...)* and your signature.

_____

_____

_____

_____

_____

_____

_____

_____

_____

_____

_____

_____

_____

_____

_____

2   En la universidad

Tema 1 ¿Qué hay?

2-1 ¿Qué hay en el salón de clase? Identify the items and people numbered in the drawings below by writing the name for each on the lines provided. Be sure to use the correct form of *a(n)* (**un, una**).

En el salón de clase, hay...

1. _____

2. _____

3. _____

4. _____

5. _____

6. _____

7. _____

8. _____

9. _____

10. _____

En el escritorio, hay...

11. _____

12. _____

13. _____

14. _____

15. _____

16. _____

2-2 En el escritorio. Complete the following nouns with the correct form of the indefinite article: **un, una, unos,** or **unas**.

1. _____ computadora   4. _____ plantas   7. _____ lápices   10. _____ profesora

2. _____ estante   5. _____ papeles   8. _____ ventanas   11. _____ profesores

3. _____ libros   6. _____ bolígrafo   9. _____ reloj   12. _____ cuaderno

Now list the numbers of the items from the preceding list that might logically be found on a desk.

_____

2-3 ¿Qué hay? Say what there is for sale and *for* (**por**) how many *dollars* (**dólares**) and *cents* (**centavos**).

MODELO   Hay **una calculadora** por **treinta y cuatro** dólares con **noventa y cinco** centavos.

MODELO   1.   2.

3.   4.   5.

1. Hay _____ por _____

   dólares con _____ centavos.

2. Hay _____ por _____ dólares.

3. Hay _____ por _____

   dólares con _____ centavos.

4. Hay _____ por _____

   dólares con _____ centavos.

5. Hay _____ por _____ centavos.

2-4 ¿Qué necesitamos hacer? Your instructor is telling the class what to do. Cross out the ending in parentheses that is not logical with the verb.

MODELO   Lean... (la pregunta – ~~un lápiz~~ – cada oración).

1. Abran... (el libro en la página 37 – la ventana y la puerta – la oración).

2. Hagan... (una silla – el ejercicio en parejas – la tarea para la próxima clase).

3. Contesten... (con oraciones completas – la siguiente pregunta – la ventana).

4. Saquen... (papel y un bolígrafo – a la pizarra – la tarea para hoy).

5. Vayan... (a la pizarra y escriban las respuestas – a la biblioteca – una calculadora).

6. Escriban... (la puerta – las preguntas con otro/a estudiante – las respuestas en la pizarra).

7. Lean... (las preguntas – las palabras en la página 64 – el estante).

8. Aprendan... (las palabras en la página 36 – el reloj – todo el vocabulario).

2-5 ¿Y tú? Answer the following questions a classmate might ask you with complete sentences in Spanish.

1. ¿Tienes otra clase los días de la clase de español?

_____

2. ¿Tienes mucha tarea en todas tus clases?

_____

3. ¿Tienes varios exámenes esta semana?

_____

2-6 Diario. Write two paragraphs. In the first paragraph, describe your classroom. Is it big or small, new or old, and pretty or ugly? What is there in the classroom? What do you generally have on your desk and in your backpack? In the second paragraph, describe your professor and the other students.

_____

_____

_____

_____

_____

_____

_____

_____

¡A escuchar!

2-7 ¿Qué hay y dónde? Listen as someone asks about where certain things are in the following illustrations. Answer each question and indicate either **a** for **el salón de clase** or **b** for **el escritorio**. You will then hear the correct answer. Listen and repeat it.

MODELO   You hear: ¿Dónde hay unos estudiantes?

               You say: **Hay unos estudiantes en el salón de clase.**

               You indicate: **a**

               You hear: Hay unos estudiantes en el salón de clase.

               You repeat: **Hay unos estudiantes en el salón de clase.**

a.

b.

1. _____   3. _____   5. _____   7. _____   9. _____

2. _____   4. _____   6. _____   8. _____   10. _____

2-8 ¿Qué necesitamos hacer? What might your instructor tell the class to do? Answer each question you hear using the cues that you see. You will then hear the correct answer. Listen and repeat it.

MODELO   You see: Contesten... con oraciones completas, por favor.

               You hear: ¿Qué necesitamos hacer con las preguntas?

               You answer: **Contesten las preguntas con oraciones completas, por favor.**

               You hear: Contesten las preguntas con oraciones completas, por favor.

               You repeat: **Contesten las preguntas con oraciones completas, por favor.**

1. Sí, hagan... en parejas, por favor.   4. Escriban... en la pizarra, por favor.

2. Abran... en la página 52, por favor.   5. Aprendan... en la página 64.

3. Lean..., por favor.   6. Escuchen y repitan...

2-9 ¿En qué orden? In random order, you will hear two commands that your instructor may give you. Connect them with **y** in the order that they would logically be done. You will then hear the correct answer. Listen and repeat it.

MODELO   You hear: Contesten con oraciones completas. / Escuchen las preguntas.

               You say: **Escuchen las preguntas y contesten con oraciones completas, por favor.**

               You hear: Escuchen las preguntas y contesten con oraciones completas, por favor.

               You repeat: **Escuchen las preguntas y contesten con oraciones completas, por favor.**

Tema 2 ¿Qué hay cerca de la universidad?

2-10 ¿Qué hay? Complete each sentence with the logical place from the list.

el estadio	el club nocturno	mi restaurante favorito	el cine	la librería	el parque

1. Hay muchos libros en español en _____.

2. Hay un partido de fútbol hoy en _____.

3. Hay buena comida en _____.

4. Hay música latina esta noche en _____.

5. Hay una película extranjera esta semana en _____.

2-11 En el centro estudiantil. Say where the students are in the student lounge with the appropriate words from the list. Use each one only once.

lejos	entre	a la izquierda	al lado	delante	detrás	encima	enfrente

MODELO   Arturo está **al lado** de la ventana.

1. Juan está _____ Daniel y Arturo.

2. Juan, Daniel y Arturo están _____ de Mari y Teresa.

3. Marta está _____ de Silvia y no hay nadie (*anybody*) a su derecha.

4. La computadora está _____ del escritorio _____ de Mari.

5. Daniel está cerca de la entrada (*entrance*) pero Ricardo está _____.

6. La entrada está _____ de Marta y Silvia.

2-12 ¿Dónde está? A student is saying where she, her parents, and her friends are at different moments. What does she say? Write sentences using the correct form of **estar** and the indefinite article **un/a** with the place.

MODELO   Mi madre **está en un gimnasio.**

1.    2.

3.    4.    5.

6.    7.

1. Mi madre _____.

2. Mis padres _____.

3. Mi novio y yo _____.

4. Mis amigos y yo _____.

5. Yo _____.

6. Mis amigos y yo _____.

7. Mi padre _____.

2-13 ¿Dónde está? A student is describing his university and where he lives. Fill in the blanks with the correct form of **estar** or **hay** (*there is* or *there are.*)

Mi apartamento (1) _____ a diez minutos de la universidad. (Yo)

(2) _____ en clase todos los días por la mañana y si (*if*)

(3) _____ mucha tarea (yo) (4) _____ en la biblioteca

por la tarde. La biblioteca (5) _____ cerca de mi clase de español y me gusta

hacer la tarea con unos amigos después de clase. (Nosotros) (6) _____ en la

biblioteca una o dos horas o a veces (nosotros) (7) _____ en un café que no

(8) _____ lejos de la universidad. (9) _____ muchos

cafés, librerías y tiendas cerca del campus y (10) _____ un cine también.

Generalmente (yo) (11) _____ en mi apartamento después de las cinco o las seis

de la tarde. Tengo dos compañeros de cuarto, pero casi nunca (12) _____ en el

apartamento hasta tarde (*until late*). Uno de ellos (13) _____ en el trabajo hasta

las diez y el otro (14) _____ en el apartamento de su novia, pero a veces su novia

y él (15) _____ aquí.

2-14 Diario. Write a paragraph similar to the one in the preceding activity, describing your own situation. Be sure to say how far your house/apartment (**casa/apartamento**) is from campus or whether your residence is on campus (**en el campus**). Tell where you are and with whom in the morning, afternoon, and evening on a typical day that you have Spanish class.

_____

_____

_____

_____

_____

_____

_____

_____

_____

_____

_____

¡A escuchar!

2-15 ¿Cómo se pronuncia? Pause the recording and underline the letter **d** in the following sentences if it is the first sound in a phrase or after the letters **n** or **l**. Then turn on the recording and listen and repeat each sentence. Note that the letter **d** is similar to the d in English where it is underlined, but it is more like the *th* of the English word *they* elsewhere.

— ¿Qué **d**ías trabaja E**d**uar**d**o?

— To**d**os los **d**ías **d**e la semana menos los sába**d**os y los **d**omingos.

— ¿**D**ón**d**e está E**d**uar**d**o to**d**o el **d**ía los sába**d**os?

— Está en el esta**d**io para un parti**d**o **d**e fútbol.

— ¿**D**ón**d**e está la tien**d**a **d**e ropa **d**onde trabaja? ¿Está a la **d**erecha o a la izquier**d**a **d**el supermerca**d**o?

— Está **d**etrás **d**el supermerca**d**o y al la**d**o **d**e un restaurante de comi**d**a italiana.

2-16 En mi cuarto. Answer each question you hear about the location of items in the following room. You will then hear the correct response. Listen and repeat it and on the illustration, write the number of each question on the item being located.

MODELO	You hear:	¿Dónde está la computadora, delante de la ventana o encima del escritorio?
	You say:	**La computadora está encima del escritorio.**
	You hear:	La computadora está encima del escritorio.
	You repeat:	**La computadora está encima del escritorio.**
	You write:	*The number of the question on the computer on the illustration.*

Tema 3 ¿Están listos o necesitan más tiempo?

2-17 ¿Cómo están? The woman from the **Modelo** is talking about her friends and family members. Complete each sentence with **estar** and the adjective from the list that best describes them. Use each adjective only once and be sure to make it agree for masculine or feminine and singular or plural.

aburrido	cansado	contento	enfermo
estupendo	interesado	listo	ocupado

MODELO   No trabajo hoy y **estoy contenta**.

1.

2.

3.

4.

5.

1. Mi hermano es un poco perezoso y siempre _____.

2. Mi compañera de clase _____.

3. Hay mucho trabajo hoy y mi padre y sus colegas _____.

   Mi padre _____ para su presentación.

4. Mis amigos y yo no _____ en la película porque no es muy

   interesante. (Nosotros) _____.

5. Mi mejor amiga y su novio _____.

2-18 ¿Dónde están? What does the woman from the preceding activity say about her friends and family members? In which blank does she use a form of **ser** and in which one **estar**?

MODELO   (Yo) **estoy** en casa hoy porque no trabajo. Hoy **es** sábado.

1. _____ las diez de la mañana y mi hermano _____
   en la cama (bed).

2. Mi compañera de clase _____ en el hospital. _____
   muy buena estudiante.

3. Mi padre y sus colegas _____ en el trabajo. _____
   muy trabajadores.

4. Mis amigos y yo _____ en el cine. _____ buenos
   amigos.

5. Mi mejor amiga no _____ muy tímida. Su novio y ella

   _____ en un club nocturno.

2-19 Nuevos amigos. Two new classmates meet each other outside of class. Complete their conversation with the correct forms of **ser** or **estar**. Remember to use **estar** to say where or with whom someone or something is or with adjectives to describe mental or physical states and conditions, and use **ser** in most other cases.

Cristina: ¡Hola! (Nosotros) (1) _____ en la misma clase de literatura, ¿no?

                  (Yo) (2) _____ Cristina.

Ana Laura: Sí, (3) _____ en la clase con la profesora Noriega, ¿verdad? (right?)

                  Mucho gusto. Me llamo Ana Laura.

Cristina: ¿De dónde (4) _____ (tú)?

Ana Laura: Originalmente, (5) _____ de Guatemala, pero ahora mi familia

                  (6) _____ en Honduras. ¿Y tú, Cristina?

Cristina: (7) _____ mexicana, de Monterrey. ¿Cómo

                  (8) _____ tus clases?

Ana Laura: Me gustan todas mis clases, pero a veces (9) _____ confundida en

                  mi clase de química. La química (10) _____ un poco difícil para mí.

Cristina: La clase de literatura (11) _____ interesante, ¿verdad?

Ana Laura: Sí, pero a veces (yo) (12) _____ cansada en la clase porque

(13) _____ a las ocho de la mañana los lunes, miércoles y viernes

y trabajo hasta las once de la noche los domingos y los jueves.

Cristina: ¿(14) _____ (tú) en la universidad todos los días?

Ana Laura: No, todas mis clases (15) _____ los lunes, miércoles y viernes.

Casi nunca (16) _____ en la universidad los martes y jueves

porque (17) _____ muy lejos de mi casa.

2-20 Mucho gusto. A student you are meeting for the first time asks you the following questions. Write the correct from of **ser** or **estar** in the first blank. Then answer each question about yourself.

1. Hola, ¿cómo _____ (tú) hoy? _____

2. ¿_____ (tú) estudiante? _____

3. ¿Qué días _____ tus clases? _____

4. ¿De dónde _____ (tú)? _____

5. ¿Cómo _____ tu apartamento (casa, residencia)? _____

_____

6. ¿_____ en el campus, cerca del campus o lejos? _____

2-21 Diario. Write a paragraph describing your classes this semester. Include the following information.

- which days you are at the university
- when each class is
- what the students and professors are like
- in which classes you are nervous, busy, bored, interested, always ready, confused, or sure of the answer
- where you are after class and at what time you are at home in the evening

_____

_____

_____

_____

_____

_____

¡A escuchar!

2-22 ¿Entienden Uds.? You will hear several things your instructor might say to a female student. Select the logical response the student might give in each case and say it aloud. You will then hear the correct response. Listen and repeat it.

MODELO   You see: a. Sí, estoy lista.   b. No sé. No estoy segura.
              You hear: ¿Cuál es la respuesta correcta?
              You indicate: **b. No sé. No estoy segura.**
              You say: **No sé. No estoy segura.**
              You hear: No sé. No estoy segura.
              You repeat: **No sé. No estoy segura.**

1. a. ¿Cuál es la tarea para mañana?   b. No, necesitamos más tiempo.

2. a. Sí, tengo una pregunta.   b. No, no estoy lista.

3. a. No comprendo.   b. ¿Qué significa **pizarra** en inglés?

4. a. ¿Cómo se escribe **tarea**?   b. No sé cómo se dice.

5. a. No sé. No comprendo la pregunta.   b. No, no necesitamos más tiempo.

6. a. Estamos confundidos. ¿Qué significa **pueden**?   b. ¿Cuál es la tarea para la próxima clase?

7. a. ¿Cómo se dice *right now* en español?   b. ¿Cuál es la tarea para hoy?

8. a. ¿Cómo se escribe **está**, con acento o sin acento?   b. No, no necesito más tiempo. Estoy lista.

2-23 ¿Cómo están y cómo son? Select the logical answer to each question you hear.

1. a. estrictos   b. bien   5. a. grande   b. en San José

2. a. bajos   b. ocupados   6. a. vieja   b. cerca de mi casa

3. a. de aquí   b. en casa   7. a. simpáticos   b. confundidos

4. a. de México   b. en mi cuarto   8. a. inteligentes b. nerviosos

2-24 ¿Y tú? Answer the following questions that another student might ask you with complete sentences in Spanish. Pause the recording in order to respond. Listen to the questions again as needed.

1. _____

2. _____

3. _____

4. _____

5. _____

Tema 4 ¿Qué te gusta hacer después de clase?

2-25 ¿Qué haces? An acquaintance is asking Alicia about her weekly activities. Complete each question and answer with the correct forms of the verb for the illustrated activity.

MODELO   — ¿**Hablas** (tú) mucho por teléfono?

— Sí, (yo) **hablo** por teléfono una o dos horas todos los días.

1.    2.    3.

1. — ¿_____ (tú) mucho la tele sola en casa los fines de semana?

— Los viernes, sí generalmente, (yo) _____ la tele porque mi novio trabaja, pero los sábados me gusta ir a bailar con él.

2. — ¿_____ bien (ustedes)?

— Yo _____ bien pero él _____ mal.

3. — A veces, ¿_____ (ustedes) algo en un café con otros amigos?

— Sí, a veces, (nosotros) _____ algo con mi hermana y su novio.

4.    5.    6.    7.

4. — ¿Tu hermano no _____ mucho tiempo contigo?

— A veces, mi hermano y su compañero de cuarto _____ los viernes conmigo, pero no mucho porque a mi novio no le gusta.

5. — ¿Tus amigos y tú _____ más música latina o más música rock?

— (Nosotros) _____ más música rock.

6. — ¿_____ (tú) mucha ropa para salir con los amigos?

— No, (yo) casi nunca _____ ropa nueva porque no tengo dinero (*money*).

7. — ¿_____ (tú) mucho en casa los fines de semana?

— Me gusta _____ en el jardín (*the garden*) los sábados por la tarde.

2-26 ¿Con frecuencia? If a student says that he is hardly ever at home on the weekend and almost always is out with friends, but that his housemate is the opposite, which adverb in parentheses does he use to describe himself and which for his housemate? Insert the adverbs in the sentences.

MODELO   Yo **casi nunca** descanso los fines de semana pero mi compañero de cuarto descansa en casa **con frecuencia**. (con frecuencia, casi nunca)

1. Mis amigos y yo _____ pasamos los sábados juntos pero sus amigos

   pasan los sábados con él _____. (casi siempre, una vez al mes)

2. Él mira la televisión _____ los viernes por la noche pero yo

   _____ miro la tele los viernes. (con frecuencia, casi nunca)

3. Yo _____ estudio los fines de semana pero él estudia

   _____. (todos los fines de semana, nunca)

4. Mis amigos y yo bailamos en un club _____, pero sus amigos

   bailan _____. (una vez a la semana, una o dos veces al año)

5. _____ yo regreso muy tarde (*late*) a casa los sábados pero él

   _____ regresa tarde a casa. (a veces, casi nunca)

2-27 En clase. Write sentences saying how often the following people do the indicated things in Spanish class. Place **(casi) siempre** and **(casi) nunca** before the verb and the other adverbs at the end of the phrase.

(casi) siempre	todos los días	con frecuencia	a veces	casi (nunca)

MODELO   (nosotros) / necesitar estudiar mucho: **Necesitamos estudiar mucho todos los días.**

1. yo / llegar tarde (*late*) a clase: _____

2. el profesor (la profesora) / hablar español: _____

_____

3. nosotros / cantar en español: _____

4. yo / escuchar bien: _____

2-28 Mis amigos y yo. Complete the following paragraph with the logical verbs from the list in the correct form. Use each verb only once, and note that some of them will not be conjugated.

comer	descansar	estar	estudiar	ir	llegar	mirar
necesitar	pasar	preparar	regresar	tocar	tomar	trabajar

Los fines de semana (yo) (1) _____ muy ocupada los viernes y sábados.

Generalmente me gusta salir con mis amigos más los sábados que los viernes. Los viernes (yo)

(2) _____ para mis clases en la biblioteca pero los sábados (yo)

(3) _____ tiempo con mi novio en un club o en un café. Mi novio

(4) _____ en un supermercado hasta las siete los sábados, pero su trabajo está a

diez minutos de mi casa y (él) siempre (5) _____ a mi casa a las siete y cuarto.

Casi siempre (nosotros) (6) _____ algo de comer en mi apartamento porque a mi

novio no le gusta (7) _____ en restaurantes. Después de comer, siempre quiero

(8) _____ a bailar a un club donde (ellos) (9) _____

música latina, pero a veces mi novio prefiere (10) _____ algo en un café con

otros amigos. A veces, (yo) (11) _____ a casa a las tres o cuatro de la mañana.

Generalmente los domingos, (yo) (12) _____ en mi apartamento porque estoy

cansada y mi compañera de cuarto y yo (13) _____ la tele. A veces (nosotras)

(14) _____ limpiar el apartamento.

2-29 Diario. Using the preceding activity as a model, write a paragraph describing your typical weekend. Stick to what you have learned how to say, and for the time being, only use non -**ar** verbs such as **ir** (to go), **salir** (to go out), or **comer** (to eat) in the infinitive after expressions like **me gusta, quiero,** or **prefiero**. You will learn how to conjugate these verbs later.

_____

_____

_____

_____

_____

_____

_____

_____

_____

_____

¡A escuchar!

2-30 ¿En clase o después de clase? Listen to each statement and indicate with **a** or **b** whether it is something done in class or after class.

a. en clase   **b. después de clase**

MODELO   You hear: Tomo algo con los amigos en un café.
            You indicate: **b**

1. _____   2. _____   3. _____   4. _____   5. _____   6. _____   7. _____   8. _____   9. _____

2-31 ¿Con qué frecuencia? You will hear the statements from the preceding activity again. Indicate how often you do each activity in or after class with the letter of the corresponding adverb.

a. siempre   **b. casi siempre**   **c. a veces**   **d. casi nunca**   **e. nunca**

MODELO   You hear: Tomo algo con los amigos en un café.

            You indicate: **c** (*that you sometimes drink something at a café with friends after class*)

1. _____   2. _____   3. _____   4. _____   5. _____   6. _____   7. _____   8. _____   9. _____

2-32 El día de Ramón. Ramón is almost always working and never has time to relax at home or enjoy himself. Select the logical adverb **a** or **b** and insert it in each sentence you hear describing his typical day. You will then hear the correct response. Listen and repeat it.

MODELO   You see: a. casi nunca   b. casi todos los días
            You hear: Ramón llega a la oficina después de las nueve.
            You indicate: **a.**
            You say: **Ramón casi nunca llega a la oficina después de las nueve.**
            You hear: Ramón casi nunca llega a la oficina después de las nueve.
            You repeat: **Ramón casi nunca llega a la oficina después de las nueve.**

1. a. casi nunca   b. casi todos los días   5. a. una vez al año   b. todos los días

2. a. nunca   b. con frecuencia   6. a. una vez al año   b. dos o tres veces al mes

3. a. casi nunca   b. todos los días   7. a. nunca   b. una vez a la semana

4. a. casi nunca   b. con frecuencia   8. a. una vez al mes   b. varias veces al mes

Tema 5 ¿Cómo pasas el día?

2-33 Los fines de semana. Complete the questions with logical words from the list.

| ¿cómo? | ¿cuándo? | ¿por qué? | ¿dónde? | ¿quién? | ¿cuál? | ¿qué? | ¿cuántos/as? |

1. — ¿_____ te gusta hacer los fines de semana generalmente?

   — Me gusta salir a comer, ir al cine o ir a bailar.

2. — ¿Con _____ te gusta salir?

   — Prefiero salir con mi amigo Daniel.

3. — ¿_____ te gusta salir con Daniel?

   — Me gusta salir con él porque es divertido y le gusta ir a bailar.

4. — ¿_____ prefieres, la comida italiana o la comida mexicana?

   — Me gustan las dos, pero prefiero la comida mexicana.

5. — ¿_____ se llama tu restaurante favorito?

   — Se llama *El Poblanito*.

6. — ¿_____ está tu restaurante favorito?

   — Está en la calle Duval.

7. — ¿_____ veces a la semana regresas a casa después de la medianoche?

   — Regreso después de la medianoche una o dos veces a la semana.

8. — ¿_____ descansas generalmente?

   — Descanso los domingos por la tarde.

2-34 ¿Y tú? How would you answer if a friend asked you each of the questions from the preceding activity? Write your answers with complete sentences.

1. _____

2. _____

3. _____

4. _____

5. _____

6. _____

7. _____

8. _____

2-35 ¿Qué o cuál? Use **cuál** in questions to say *what* with the verb **ser** if you are making a selection out of a group of possibilities. Use **qué** to say *what* with verbs other than **ser,** or with **ser** if you are asking for a definition. Complete the following questions with **qué** or **cuál**.

1. ¿_____ te gusta hacer con tus amigos?

2. ¿_____ es tu día favorito para salir con los amigos?

3. ¿_____ es el mejor restaurante cerca de la universidad?

4. ¿_____ prefieres comer en un restaurante de comida mexicana?

5. ¿_____ significa la palabra *tienda* en inglés?

6. ¿_____ es una buena tienda para comprar ropa?

7. ¿Sabes (*Do you know*) _____ es una zapatería?

8. ¿_____ quieres hacer este fin de semana?

2-36 ¿Y tú? Imagine a friend is asking you each of the questions from the preceding activity. Answer each one with a complete sentence in Spanish.

1. _____

2. _____

3. _____

4. _____

5. _____

6. _____

7. _____

8. _____

2-37 ¿Cuál es la pregunta? Complete the following conversations with the logical questions. The first question has been done as an example.

1. — **¿Dónde está Lorenzo?**

   — Está en su cuarto.

   — _____

   — No baila con nadie (*with anyone*). Baila solo.

   — _____

   — Baila muy mal.

   Lorenzo

2. — _____

   — Estudia con Aura.

   — _____

   — Están en la biblioteca.

   — _____

   — Estudian historia.

   — _____

   — Estudian porque hay un examen el lunes.

   Patricio y Aura

2-38 Diario. Write an e-mail to a Spanish speaker you have met on the Internet. Describe some of your activities on the weekend and ask him/her the same information, using at least five different question words. You may begin the message with **Hola** and any name you wish.

_____

_____

_____

_____

_____

_____

_____

_____

_____

¡A escuchar!

2-39 Preguntas. You will hear an answer to a question about the party in the following illustration. Using the logical question word from those provided, ask the question that elicited the answer. You will then hear the correct answer. Listen and repeat it, then indicate the question word used.

MODELO   You hear: Alberto toca la guitarra.
           You see: a. qué   b. cuándo
           You say: **¿Qué toca Alberto?**
           You hear: ¿Qué toca Alberto?
           You repeat: **¿Qué toca Alberto?**
           You indicate: **a.**

1. a. quién   b. cuánta   4. a. dónde   b. cómo   7. a. cuánta   b. qué

2. a. por qué b. dónde   5. a. por qué b. con quién   8. a. dónde   b. cuántos

3. a. por qué b. cuál   6. a. quiénes b. por qué   9. a. cuántas   b. cómo

¡Trato hecho!

2-40 En la red. On the Internet, find the homepage of a university in a Spanish-speaking country by doing a search for *universidades en México, universidades en España,* or *universidades en* followed by the name of another Hispanic country where you would like to study. Write the address of the site you consult below, and look for the information that follows.

www. _____

1. List the headings you find on the menu bar and what you think they are in English.

   _____

   _____

   _____

2. What **departamentos** or **facultades** are there at the university? Put an *X* next to any that are not found at your university.

   _____

   _____

   _____

3. What three facts can you find and understand about the admission process?

   _____

   _____

   _____

4. What information can you find about the location of the campus and/or lodging for students?

   _____

   _____

   _____

5. What information can you find about extracurricular activities, such as sports, at the university?

   _____

   _____

2-41 Composición. Using what you have learned in this chapter, write a composition describing what there is at or near your university or in your city, and what you and your friends do after class or on the weekend and how often. Be sure to explain where each place that you mention is located. Also tell when you are busy, tired, bored, or happy, and why. You may incorporate what you wrote in your ***Diarios*** as appropriate.

_____

_____

_____

_____

_____

_____

_____

_____

_____

_____

_____

_____

_____

_____

_____

_____

_____

_____

3 En casa

Tema 1 ¿Dónde vives? ¿Cuál es tu dirección?

3-1 ¿Qué hay en la casa? Label as many items as you can in the house below. Be sure to use the correct form of *a(n)* (**un, una**) or *some* (**unos, unas**). A few have been done as examples.

1. _____

2. _____

3. _____ una cocina _____

4. _____

5. _____

6. _____

7. _____

8. _____

9. _____

10. _____

11. _____ una chimenea _____

12. _____

13. _____

14. _____

15. _____

16. _____

17. _____

18. _____ un jardín _____

19. _____

20. _____ una flor _____

3-2 La cocina está... Now indicate where the rooms or the items from the house in the preceding activity are placed in relation to other rooms or objects.

MODELO   La estufa está al lado del **microondas**.

1. El microondas está a la izquierda de la _____.

2. El dormitorio está al lado del _____.

3. El televisor está delante del _____.

4. El comedor está al lado de la _____.

5. La piscina está en el centro del _____.

6. El sofá está en la _____.

3-3 Dinero internacional. Spell out the numbers in parentheses that indicate the amount of American dollars you receive in exchange for currencies from different Hispanic countries.

1. _____ (100) euros son

   _____ (126) dólares americanos.

2. _____ (400) pesos argentinos son

   _____ (135) dólares americanos.

3. _____ (6.000.000) de bolívares venezolanos son

   _____ (3.130) dólares americanos.

4. _____ (7000) colones costarricenses son

   _____ (800) dólares americanos.

5. _____ (900) quetzales guatemaltecos son

   _____ (115) dólares americanos.

3-4 ¿Cuánto pagas? Write out the numbers in parentheses in the following conversations.

1. — ¿Cuánto es la cuenta de la luz (*electric bill*)?

   — Pago más o menos _____ (100) dólares al mes.

2. — ¿Cuánto pagas por los libros cada semestre?

   — Pago entre _____ (250) y _____ (300) dólares generalmente.

3. — ¿Cuánto pagas de alquiler?

— Pago _____ (1600) dólares al mes por mi apartamento.

4. — ¿Cuánto pagan para estudiar en la universidad?

— Pagamos _____ (5500) dólares cada semestre.

3-5 ¿Y tú? Answer the following questions a classmate might ask you with complete sentences in Spanish.

1. ¿Cuántos estudiantes hay en la universidad?

_____

2. ¿Cuánto pagas para estudiar en la universidad cada año?

_____

3. ¿Cuál es tu dirección?

_____

4. ¿Cuántos habitantes hay en tu ciudad aproximadamente?

_____

3-6 Diario. Write two paragraphs. In the first paragraph, describe your parents' house. How many rooms are in the house? Where are the different rooms located? Is there a yard or a garden? Is there a garage? In the second paragraph, describe your room or apartment at the university or your room at home if you live with your parents. If applicable, say if it is expensive and how much you pay. Do you like where you live? If not, where would you like to live instead?

_____

_____

_____

_____

_____

_____

_____

_____

¡A escuchar!

3-7 Anuncios. Complete the following classified ads for apartments with the information that you hear regarding the number of rooms and the price of the apartment. Write any numbers using numerals.

1. Bonito apartamento en el segundo piso. Tres dormitorios, dos baños en excelentes condiciones. El

   complejo tiene _____ y cancha de tenis. _____
   dólares al mes. Teléfono: (787) 640-5823.

2. Apartamento agradable y muy céntrico. Un dormitorio y un _____. A cinco

   minutos del centro. _____ al mes. Incluye agua y luz. Teléfono: (939) 644-3499.

3. Precioso apartamento, tres cuartos, un baño, _____, sala,

   _____, balcón. Situado en Carolina, cerca de Plaza Carolina. Acceso

   controlado. Precio mensual: _____. Para más información: (787) 531-7004.

4. Apartamento amueblado, dos _____, dos baños, terraza. Cerca de la piscina,

   cancha de tenis y playa. En excelentes condiciones. _____ al mes. Teléfono:
   (787) 864-7667.

3-8 ¿Dónde vives? Listen as a classmate talks about where he lives. Indicate whether the statements are also true about where you live by marking either **a. cierto** or **b. falso**. Then pause the recording and write a sentence indicating that the statement is true for you too, or change the statement to make it true for you.

MODELO	You hear:	Vivo en la calle Fuencarral.
	You indicate:	**a. cierto** You write: **Vivo en la calle Fuencarral también (*also*).**
	Or:	**b. falso** You write: **Vivo en la calle Huxley.**

1. a. cierto   b. falso _____

2. a. cierto   b. falso _____

3. a. cierto   b. falso _____

4. a. cierto   b. falso _____

5. a. cierto   b. falso _____

6. a. cierto   b. falso _____

7. a. cierto   b. falso _____

8. a. cierto   b. falso _____

Tema 2 ¿Cómo es tu cuarto?

3-9 ¿Qué hay? Look at the illustration below and complete each sentence with the logical word.

1. La lámpara está encima de la _____.

2. La alfombra está en el _____.

3. La _____ está a la izquierda de la computadora.

4. El gato está encima de la _____.

5. Hay un espejo en la _____.

6. Hay un _____ encima del televisor.

7. La silla está delante del _____.

8. Hay una _____ a la derecha de la computadora.

3-10 De colores. What colors are the following flags (**banderas**)? Look them up if you don't know.

1. La bandera norteamericana es roja, blanca y _____.

2. La bandera española es roja y _____.

3. La bandera mexicana es roja, _____ y blanca.

4. La bandera puertorriqueña es roja, azul y _____.

5. La bandera colombiana es amarilla, _____ y roja.

6. La bandera peruana es _____ y blanca.

3-11 El cuarto de Juan y el cuarto de Mario. Compare Juan's and Mario's rooms and complete the following sentences based on what you see in the illustrations.

el cuarto de Juan   el cuarto de Mario

MODELO   El cuarto de Juan está ordenado pero el cuarto de Mario está **desordenado**.

1. En el cuarto de Mario su ropa está en el suelo pero en el cuarto de Juan su ropa está en el

_____.

2. En el cuarto de Juan sus libros están en el _____ pero en el cuarto de Mario sus libros están en el suelo.

3. En el cuarto de Juan hay un perro pero en el cuarto de Mario hay tres _____.

4. En el cuarto de Juan no hay nada encima de su cama pero en el cuarto de Mario hay cosas por todos

_____.

5. En el cuarto de Juan no hay nada en la pared pero en el cuarto de Mario hay dos

_____ en la pared.

6. El cuarto de Juan está _____ pero el cuarto de Mario está sucio.

Now for each of the preceding statements, say whether your room is more like Juan's room or Mario's room at the moment.

MODELO   Mi cuarto está desordenado como el cuarto de Mario.

1. _____

2. _____

3. _____

4. _____

5. _____

6. _____

3-12 ¿Qué tienen? Complete the following sentences with the appropriate form of **tener** and the logical possessive adjective.

MODELO   **Mis** compañeros de casa y yo **tenemos** que compartir un apartamento en las afueras, porque el centro es muy caro.

1. _____ amigos y yo _____ un apartamento grande y agradable.

2. Uno de mis compañeros de casa _____ en la sala

   _____ reproductor de DVD y miramos películas.

3. Mis otros compañeros de casa _____   _____

   dormitorios desordenados, pero yo _____   _____ dormitorio limpio.

4. También nosotros _____ un gato. _____ gato se llama Nicolás.

3-13 ¿Y tú? Answer the following questions a classmate might ask you with complete sentences in Spanish.

1. ¿Vives con alguien? _____

2. ¿Tienes un cuarto grande? _____

3. ¿Qué cosas hay en tu cuarto? _____

   _____

4. ¿Te gusta tu cuarto? ¿Por qué? _____

   _____

3-14 Diario. Write a paragraph describing your Spanish classroom. Is it big or small, new or old, pretty or ugly? How many students are in the class? What color are the walls, the door, the blackboard? What items are there in the classroom and where are they?

_____

_____

_____

_____

_____

_____

¡A escuchar!

3-15 En mi cuarto hay... Identify the items that the person in the recording has in his room at the university.

__X__ una alfombra   _____ una cómoda   _____ un espejo   _____ muebles bonitos

_____ un televisor   _____ una computadora   _____ una lámpara   _____ libros en el suelo

_____ pinturas   _____ dos ventanas   _____ estantes   _____ un perro

3-16 ¿Cierto? Listen as a classmate talks about where she lives. Indicate whether the statements are also true about where you live by marking either **a. cierto** or **b. falso**. Then pause the recording and write a sentence indicating that the statement is true for you too, or change the statement to make it true for you.

MODELO   You hear: Mi coche es rojo.
                     You indicate: **a. cierto**   You write: **Mi coche es rojo también.**
                     Or: **b. falso**   You write: **Mi coche es gris.** _or_ **No tengo coche.**

1. a. cierto   b. falso _____

2. a. cierto   b. falso _____

3. a. cierto   b. falso _____

4. a. cierto   b. falso _____

5. a. cierto   b. falso _____

6. a. cierto   b. falso _____

3-17 Mi compañero. Listen to some questions a person is being asked about his roommate. Answer each question you hear by completing the cues that you see. You will then hear the correct answer. Listen and repeat it, and write the missing words in the blanks. Stop the recording if necessary.

MODELO   You see: No, no vivo solo, tengo un _____.
                     You hear: ¿Vives solo?
                     You answer: **No, no vivo solo, tengo un compañero de casa.**
                     You hear: No, no vivo solo, tengo un compañero de casa.
                     You repeat and write: No, no vivo solo, tengo un **compañero de casa.**

1. Sí, mi compañero de casa y yo _____ una casa en las afueras.

2. Sí, en nuestra sala tenemos un _____ y un _____.

3. No, nuestra casa no está generalmente _____.

4. Sí, en nuestra casa hay libros _____.

5. No, yo no _____, pero mi compañero tiene un _____ nuevo.

6. Sí, tenemos una sala para estudiar, con un _____ y una _____.

Tema 3 ¿Cómo es tu familia?

3-18 La familia de Alicia. Help Alicia label her family tree by writing in the correct name for each relationship.

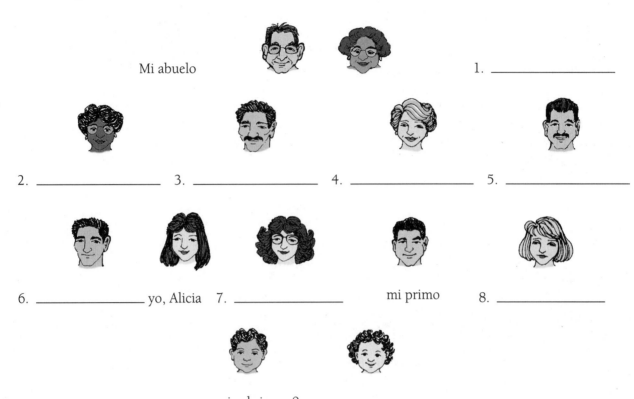

Mi abuelo

1. _____

2. _____   3. _____   4. _____   5. _____

6. _____ yo, Alicia   7. _____   mi primo   8. _____

mi sobrino   9. _____

3-19 Mi familia. Complete the following description that Germán gives about his family by selecting the logical options from those provided in parentheses.

¡Hola! (1) _____ (Éste es / Me llamo) Germán y

(2) _____ (soy / tengo) doce años. En mi familia somos ocho y Gazpacho. Mi

padre y mi (3) _____ (madre / profesor), mis tres

(4) _____ (perros / hermanas), Lucía, Lidia y Sonia, mis dos

(5) _____ (hermanos / vecinos), Javi y Ernesto, y mi

(6) _____ (árbol / gato), Gazpacho. No tengo

(7) _____ (abuelos / hermanos), pero tengo seis

(8) _____ (tíos / solteros). Dos de mis tíos están

(9) _____ (rubios / casados) y tienen (10) _____

(hijos / mayor). Todos mis hermanos (11) _____ (se llaman / se parecen) a mi

madre en el aspecto físico pero no (12) _____ (de estatura media / en el

carácter). Mi madre es una persona muy especial.

3-20 ¿Cómo son? Complete the following statements.

el primo Eduardo

el abuelo Francisco

el tío Emilio

la prima Rosa

MODELO   **El abuelo Francisco** es viejo.

1. _____ usa gafas.

2. _____ tiene bigote.

3. _____ tiene el pelo largo.

4. _____ es de mediana edad.

5. _____ , _____ y

   _____ tienen el pelo corto.

6. _____ es joven.

3-21 Contrarios. Answer the following questions in the negative, using the antonym of the adjective.

MODELO   — ¿Tiene una familia grande?
            — No, **tiene una familia pequeña.**

1. — ¿Tienen una hermana mayor?

   — No, _____.

2. — ¿Es alto el padre de René?

   — No, _____.

3. — ¿Tiene unos abuelos viejos?

   — No, _____.

4. — ¿Es Adriana mejor que su hermano en matemáticas?

   — No, _____.

5. — ¿Está gorda la tía de Antonio?

   — No, _____.

3-22 Quiero tener clases mejores. Answer the following questions a classmate might ask you about your ideal classes, making comparisons with the classes that you have now.

MODELO   ¿Quieres tener clases agradables?
               Quiero tener clases más agradables que ahora. *or*
               Quiero tener clases tan agradables como ahora.

1. ¿Quieres tener clases interesantes?

_____

2. ¿Quieres tener clases grandes?

_____

3. ¿Quieres tener tarea en tus clases?

_____

4. ¿Quieres tener profesores buenos?

_____

3-23 Diario. Write a paragraph comparing your family and your best friend's family. How many members do you have in your families? Are they similar? How are they different?

_____

_____

_____

_____

_____

_____

_____

_____

_____

_____

_____

_____

¡A escuchar!

3-24 La familia de Pablo. Listen to a description of Pablo's family and fill in the missing words. Listen again as necessary.

Tengo una familia (1) _____. Mis padres (2) _____ Julia y

Alejandro, mi hermana (3) _____ se llama Ana, y mi hermano

(4) _____ se llama Julio. En el aspecto (5) _____, Ana

(6) _____ mucho a mi madre, pero tiene el pelo más

(7) _____. Julio es más (8) _____ que mi padre y menos

(9) _____ que yo. En el (10) _____ somos todos diferentes.

3-25 No es lógico. Change the following comparisons so that they are more logical. You will then hear the correct answer. Listen and say it again.

MODELO   You hear: Generalmente los tíos son mayores que los abuelos.

                You say: **Generalmente los tíos son menores que los abuelos.**

                You hear: Generalmente los tíos son menores que los abuelos.

                You repeat: **Generalmente los tíos son menores que los abuelos.**

3-26 Juan y Mario. A new acquaintance has Juan and Mario confused. Look at the illustrations below and listen to the descriptions of Juan and Mario. Say the opposite using the cues. You will then hear the correct answer. Listen and repeat and fill in the blanks with the missing words.

              Juan, 22 años   **Mario, 21 años**

MODELO   You see: No, Juan es _____ que Mario.

              You hear: Juan es menos serio que Mario.

              You say: **No, Juan es más serio que Mario.**

              You hear: No, Juan es más serio que Mario.

              You repeat and write: No, Juan es **más serio** que Mario.

1. No, Juan es _____ que Mario.

2. No, Mario es _____ que Juan.

3. No, Mario es _____ que Juan.

4. No, el coche de Juan es _____ que el coche de Mario.

5. No, Mario tiene el pelo _____ que Juan.

6. No, Juan es _____ que Mario.

Tema 4 ¿Qué haces los días de clase?

3-27 ¿Qué hace Ángela? Describe Ángela's day by filling in the verb for the illustrated activity in the form for **ella,** unless another subject is stated. Use the verbs presented on page 80 of the textbook.

Por la mañana   Por la tarde

1.    2.    3.    4.

Por la noche

5.    6.    7.

1. Generalmente Ángela _____ sola en casa por la mañana, pero a veces sus

   amigas del trabajo y ella _____ en un restaurante antes de ir al trabajo.

2. Casi siempre _____ el periódico después de comer.

3. Generalmente _____ sola en el parque por la mañana, pero a veces unos

   amigos _____ con ella.

4. Por la tarde, Ángela _____ a sus clases, pero cuando no tiene clase ella y sus

   compañeros _____ el vocabulario para su clase de italiano.

5. Por la noche _____ con sus amigos a veces, pero a veces sus padres

   _____ con ella.

6. Generalmente, Ángela _____ y _____ su correo
   electrónico por la noche.

7. Por la noche, Ángela _____ una película, pero a veces sus amigos y ella

_____ un vídeo juntos (*together*).

3-28 Los días de clase. Complete the following paragraph about Paco´s routine by selecting the appropriate verbs from the list. The verbs need to be conjugated in the first person (**yo**).

asistir	correr	comer	aprender	escribir	leer	ver	beber

Por la mañana, (1) _____ solo generalmente.

(2) _____ el periódico y (3) _____ café. Por la tarde,

(4) _____ a mis clases y (5) _____ el vocabulario para

mi clase de español. En la biblioteca (6) _____ ensayos y

(7) _____ mi correo electrónico. Por la noche,

(8) _____ en el parque.

3-29 ¿Con qué frecuencia? Answer the following questions a friend might ask you indicating how often you do the activities mentioned, using **(casi) siempre, a veces,** or **(casi) nunca**.

1. ¿Asistes a tus clases?

_____

2. ¿Corres en el parque los días de clase?

_____

3. ¿Escribes ensayos para tus clases?

_____

4. ¿Ves vídeos para tu clase de español?

_____

5. ¿Lees el periódico por la mañana?

_____

6. ¿Comes pizza por la noche?

_____

3-30 No comprendemos. Sue and Michael are having difficulties in their Spanish class and are talking to their professor. Complete their conversation logically with the **nosotros** or **ustedes** forms of the verbs from the list below.

| escribir | leer | creer | aprender | comprender | deber | ver | asistir |

Sue y Michael: No (1) _____ los vídeos que

(2) _____ en clase.

El profesor: ¿(3) _____ a clase cada día?

Sue y Michael: No, no asistimos a clase todos los días y a veces no (4) _____

el vocabulario del libro.

El profesor: ¿(5) _____ los ensayos para la clase?

Sue y Michael: A veces no escribimos los ensayos, pero (6) _____ el

periódico en español. ¿Qué debemos hacer para comprender más?

El profesor: (7) _____ aprender todo el vocabulario y escribir los ensayos

para la clase siempre. Ustedes (8) _____ que la clase de

español no es difícil y no trabajan mucho, pero necesitan trabajar más.

3-31 Diario. Write two paragraphs comparing your activities with those of your parents during the week. In the first paragraph, describe your own daily routine in the morning, afternoon, and evening using the verbs presented on page 80 of the textbook. In the second paragraph, describe your parents' daily routine in the morning, afternoon, and evening.

_____

_____

_____

_____

_____

_____

_____

_____

¡A escuchar!

3-32 ¿Cómo se pronuncia? Pause the recording and underline the letter **b** or **v** in the following sentences if it is the first sound after a pause or after the letters **m** or **n**. Then turn on the recording and listen and repeat each sentence. Note that the letters **b** and **v** are pronounced the same, and they are similar to the *b* in English where they are underlined, pronounced with both lips pressed tightly against each other. In other positions, they are still pronounced with the two lips, but they are not pressed as tightly together.

— **Vi**v**o en una casa cerca de la uni**v**ersidad.

— Escri**b**o correos electrónicos con **b**astante frecuencia.

— Me gusta mi **b**arrio. Hay **v**ecinos **b**uenos, un parque y muchos cafés.

— **B**e**b**o café por las mañanas, **v**eo la tele**v**isión por las tardes.

— **V**endo mis li**b**ros en **v**erano (*summer*) después del final del semestre.

3-33 ¿En clase o después de clase? Listen to each statement and indicate with **a** or **b** whether it is something done **en clase** or **después de clase**.

a. en clase   **b. después de clase**

MODELO   You hear: Comemos con amigos.
                 You indicate: **b**

1. _____   2. _____   3. _____   4. _____   5. _____   6. _____

7. _____   8. _____   9. _____   10. _____   11. _____   12. _____

3-34 A veces... Answer the following questions a friend might ask you with complete sentences in Spanish.

MODELO   You hear: ¿Corres en el parque con frecuencia?
                 You write: **Sí, corro en el parque todos los días.** *or* **No, nunca corro en el parque.**
                 or **Corro en el parque a veces/con frecuencia.**

1. _____

2. _____

3. _____

4. _____

5. _____

6. _____

7. _____

8. _____

Tema 5 ¿Qué haces los sábados?

3-35 Los días de semana o los fines de semana. Say whether the activities listed are things students generally do at the university during the week (**los días de semana**) or during their free time on weekends (**los fines de semana**).

MODELO   hacer un viaje a la playa: **Hacen un viaje a la playa los fines de semana.**

1. comer con amigos en la cafetería: _____

2. asistir a clase: _____

3. salir a bailar: _____

4. asistir a un concierto: _____

5. traer preguntas a la clase: _____

6. salir al cine: _____

7. correr en el parque después de clase: _____

3-36 Los fines de semana de Elena. Describe what Elena does on Saturday with a verb or expression presented on page 86 of the textbook.

1.

2.

3.

4.

5.

1. Generalmente Elena _____ sola los sábados, pero a veces sus

   amigos _____ con ella.

2. A veces Elena y sus amigos _____, pero a veces ella está

   cansada y no _____.

3. Los sábados Elena pone un CD y _____ música.

4. Generalmente, los sábados Elena y sus amigos _____ a un bar, pero a veces

   Elena _____ una fiesta en su casa.

5. A veces Elena y sus amigos _____ a la montaña los sábados,

   pero a veces Elena _____ sola a la playa.

3-37 Los sábados de Andrés. Complete the following paragraph where Andrés describes what he usually does on Saturdays. Select a verb from the list below and conjugate it appropriately. You may use the same verb twice.

asistir	hacer	leer	poner	ver	salir

Los sábados generalmente yo (1) _____ con mis amigos. Nosotros

(2) _____ a un concierto o (3) _____ una película. A

veces también yo (4) _____ un viaje con mi familia a la playa. Si estoy cansado,

paso mucho tiempo en casa y (5) _____ música o (6) _____

una revista o un buen libro. A veces mis amigos y yo (7) _____ ejercicio los

sábados o (8) _____ a un restaurante.

3-38 ¿Cuál es la pregunta? Write the logical question for each of the following answers. The italicized words will help you determine which question word to use.

MODELO   **¿Dónde haces ejercicio?**
           Hago ejercicio *en la sala.*

1. _____

   Generalmente, bebo *poco* café.

2. _____

   Asisto a conciertos con amigos *los sábados por la noche* generalmente.

3. _____

   Los fines de semana hago mi tarea *los domingos por la noche* generalmente.

4. _____

   Generalmente, oigo *mucha* música.

5. _____

   Generalmente escribo *pocos* correos electrónicos.

6. _____

Los fines de semana hago viajes *con frecuencia*.

7. _____

A veces pongo música para bailar en mi dormitorio.

8. _____

Generalmente veo la televisión *por la mañana*.

3-39 ¿Y tú? Now answer the questions from the preceding exercise saying what you do.

1. _____

2. _____

3. _____

4. _____

5. _____

6. _____

7. _____

8. _____

3-40 Diario. Write a paragraph describing what you do on Saturdays. Do you go out with your friends? Do you spend a lot of time at home? What do you do when you stay at home? Use the verbs presented on page 84 of the textbook or others that you have learned.

_____

_____

_____

_____

_____

_____

_____

_____

¡A escuchar!

3-41 ¿Cómo se pronuncia? Pause the recording and underline the letter **g** in the following sentences if it is pronounced like the Spanish letter **j**. Then turn on the recording and listen and repeat each sentence. Note that this pronunciation of the Spanish **g** is similar to a harsh English *h* sound pronounced with the tongue arched high in the back of the mouth.

— Mi **g**ato está encima del **g**araje.

— En **g**eneral, comprendo las pre**g**untas del profesor de in**g**lés.

— Mi clase favorita es la clase de biolo**g**ía con la profesora **G**arcía.

— **G**ermán es el mejor estudiante de la clase.

— Sal**g**o al cine con mis ami**g**os los sábados.

— A veces ha**g**o un viaje con **G**ema a la playa.

3-42 ¿Qué hacemos el sábado? Listen to a conversation between two friends, Marta and Antonio, who don't agree on what they want to do next Saturday. List the activities that Marta wants to do under **Marta quiere...**, and the activities that Antonio wants to do under **Antonio quiere...** .

Marta quiere...	**Antonio quiere...**
_____	_____
_____	_____
_____	_____
_____	_____

3-43 Preguntas. Listen to the questions one friend asks another. Answer each question by supplying the logical verb. When you hear the verification, listen and repeat the correct answer and write the missing word in the blank.

MODELO	You see:	No, no _____ con Antonio el sábado.
	You hear:	¿Sales con Antonio el sábado?
	You say:	**No, no salgo con Antonio el sábado.**
	You hear:	No, no salgo con Antonio el sábado.
	You repeat and write:	**No, no <u>salgo</u> con Antonio el sábado.**

1. Sí, _____ una fiesta en mi casa el sábado por la noche.

2. No, no _____ música latina.

3. Sí, mis amigos _____ discos compactos de música latina.

4. Sí, mis padres _____ un viaje el sábado.

5. No, no _____ la televisión en la fiesta.

Nombre: _____ Fecha: _____

¡Trato hecho!

3-44 En la red. On the Internet, search for information on household and family structure among Hispanics. Begin by searching for *U.S. Hispanic household and family structure*. Check the sites you find for the information requested below and answer the questions in English. Write down the addresses of the interesting and useful sites you discover and share them with your instructor and other students.

Addresses of useful and interesting sites:

www._____

www._____

www._____

1. Which type of household predominates among Hispanics in the U.S.? What factors might contribute to change this situation in the future?

_____

_____

_____

2. What are the trends in marital status of Hispanics living in the U.S.? Are they expected to change?

_____

_____

_____

3. What language predominates in Hispanic households? What is the common language of communication outside the family environment?

_____

_____

_____

3-45 Composición. Using what you have learned in this chapter, write a composition describing the place where you live while you are at school. Explain also if you live alone or with roommates or family, and compare how your rooms are. Then describe what you generally do when you are home on the weekend. You may incorporate what you wrote in your **Diarios** as appropriate.

_____

_____

_____

_____

_____

_____

_____

_____

_____

_____

_____

_____

_____

_____

_____

_____

_____

_____

_____

_____

4   En los ratos libres

Tema 1 ¿Adónde vas en tus ratos libres?

4-1 ¿Adónde van? Using the subjects given, explain or ask where people go to do the pictured activities.

MODELO   Ellos **van a un club nocturno.**

1.    2.    3.    4.

5.    6.    7.

1. Mis amigos y yo _____.

2. Mis amigos _____.

3. ¿(Tú) _____?

4. ¿(Ustedes) _____?

5. (Yo) _____.

6. (Nosotros) _____.

7. ¿(Tú) _____?

4-2 ¿Y ustedes? Complete the following sentences saying how often you and your acquaintances go to the place mentioned in the item with the same number in the preceding activity.

con frecuencia	a veces	una vez a la semana	dos veces al mes	(casi) nunca

MODELO   Mis amigos **casi nunca van a un club nocturno. /**
Mis amigos **van a un club nocturno dos o tres veces al mes.**

1. Mis padres _____.

2. Yo _____.

3. Mi mejor amigo/a _____.

4. Mi mejor amigo/a y yo _____.

5. Mi madre _____.

6. Mis amigos y yo _____.

7. Mis vecinos _____.

4-3 ¿Qué hacen allí? Explain why the following people go to the indicated places with the logical reason from the list.

MODELO   nosotros / el laboratorio de lenguas
Nosotros vamos al laboratorio de lenguas para escuchar el CD de español.

comer   tomar algo   descansar   aprender a hablar español
escuchar el CD de español   levantar pesas   trabajar

1. nosotros / la clase de español

_____

2. mis padres / el trabajo

_____

3. muchos estudiantes / la cafetería

_____

4. algunos (some) estudiantes / el gimnasio

_____

5. después de clase, yo / mi casa

_____

6. a veces, mis amigos y yo / café

_____

4-4 Entrevista. Complete the following questions another student might ask you with the appropriate form of **ir**. Then answer each question with a complete sentence in Spanish.

1. ¿Qué días _____ (Uds.) a la clase de español?

   _____

2. ¿Adónde _____ (tú) generalmente después de la clase de español?

   _____

3. Cuando sales con los amigos los fines de semana, ¿adónde _____ (Uds.) generalmente?

   _____

4. ¿Quién _____ al café con más frecuencia, tú o tu mejor amigo/a?

   _____

5. ¿Adónde _____ tus amigos y tú para descansar y hablar?

   _____

4-5 Diario. Write two paragraphs. In the first one, say where you generally go on the days you have Spanish class and in the second, talk about where you go on Saturdays. Be sure to tell at what time you go to each place and with whom, if you are not alone. Remember to use **ir** to say *to go,* but **salir** if you want to say *to go out.*

_____

_____

_____

_____

_____

_____

_____

_____

_____

_____

¡A escuchar!

4-6 ¿Por qué no vamos a...? Listen as someone says what he feels like doing and suggest going with him to one of the places listed. Then listen and repeat as you hear the correct answer and write the number of the question in the blank next to the place suggested.

MODELO   You hear: Tengo ganas de ver la exposición de arte medieval.

                You suggest: **¿Por qué no vamos al museo de arte?**

                You hear: ¿Por qué no vamos al museo de arte?

                You repeat: **¿Por qué no vamos al museo de arte?**

                You indicate: *The number of the question next to **el museo de arte.***

_____ el centro comercial   _____ un club

_____ el gimnasio   _____ la montaña

_____ **Modelo** _____ el museo de arte   _____ el lago

_____ el parque   _____ el café

_____ el cine   _____ la casa

4-7 Planes. Listen to a conversation in which a couple discusses their plans today and complete the following sentences according to the dialogue.

1. Ella va _____ porque tiene que _____ algunas cosas.

2. Ella no tiene mucho tiempo porque (ellos) _____ esta tarde.

3. Después de eso, (ellos) van a ir _____ porque él quiere ver una

_____.

4. Van a comer en un restaurante de comida mexicana que está _____.

4-8 Entrevista. Answer the following questions another student might ask you with complete sentences in Spanish.

1. _____

2. _____

3. _____

4. _____

5. _____

Tema 2 ¿Qué tiempo hace? ¿Qué vas a hacer?

4-9 ¿Qué tiempo hace? You and some of your acquaintances are going on a trip to South America in late July and you are checking how the weather is. Complete the sentences with the correct form of **ir,** the country from the map, and a word describing the weather from the list.

sol	mal	calor	frío	fresco	viento	nublado	llueve	nieva

MODELO   Mis padres **van** a **Venezuela**. Allí hace mucho **calor** hoy.

1. Mis hermanos y yo _____

   a _____.

   Allí hace _____ generalmente.

2. Yo también _____

   a _____.

   Hoy el cielo está _____.

3. Mis hermanos _____ a

   _____. Necesitan paraguas

   (*umbrellas*) porque allí _____.

4. ¿Quién _____ a

   _____? Allí no hace tanto frío

   ahora, sino (*but, rather*) _____.

5. Nadie _____ a _____.

   En julio, a veces hace mucho _____.

6. Y tú, ¿_____ a _____ con tu familia?

   Dicen que hace mucho _____ a veces en julio.

7. ¿_____ Uds. a _____ también?

   Pueden (*You can*) esquiar porque _____.

8. ¿Por qué quieres _____ a _____?

   El cielo está _____ y hace muy _____ tiempo ahora.

4-10 Los meses. Complete the following conversation between Pilar, a foreign-exchange student from Chile, and Heather, the youngest member of her American family.

Heather: Aquí en Estados Unidos, los meses de otoño son (1) _____,

(2) _____ y noviembre.

Pilar: En Chile, (3) _____, (4) _____ y mayo son los meses de otoño.

Heather: Mi estación favorita es el verano durante los meses de junio,

(5) _____ y (6) _____.

Pilar: Es invierno durante esos meses en Chile. Los meses de verano son

(7) _____, (8) _____ y febrero.

4-11 ¿Cuándo nacieron? Write sentences saying when each of these people was born (**nació**). Note that in Spanish the day is given before the month when writing dates with numerals.

MODELO Antonio Banderas (10/8/60) **nació el diez de agosto del año mil novecientos sesenta.**

1. Jennifer López (24/7/70): _____

2. Salma Hayek (2/9/68): _____

3. Sammy Sosa (12/11/68): _____

4-12 ¿Qué van a hacer? Use **ir a** + *infinitive* with a phrase from the list to say what is going to happen if the weather is as indicated. Use each item from the list only once.

esquiar	necesitar mi paraguas (*umbrella*)	llover	nevar	ir al parque	tomar el sol en la playa

MODELO Si hace muy buen tiempo, todos **vamos a ir al parque.**

1. Si hace sol y calor este fin de semana, (nosotros) _____.

2. Si llueve esta tarde, (yo) _____.

3. Si está muy nublado, pero no hace frío, _____.

4. Si nieva mucho este invierno, (nosotros) _____.

5. Si no hace frío este invierno, no _____.

4-13 ¿Cuándo? Say when you are going to do the pictured activities the next time.

MODELO   **Voy a ver la tele esta noche. / Voy a ver la tele este fin de semana. / No sé cuándo voy a ver la tele.**

1.   2.   3.   4.

1. _____

2. _____

3. _____

4. _____

4-14 Diario. Write a paragraph talking about your plans for this weekend. First, say how the weather is going to be, according to the weather forecast. Then give your plans for Friday night and Saturday and Sunday morning, afternoon, and evening. If your plans depend on the weather, say what you are going to do under different conditions.

_____

_____

_____

_____

_____

_____

_____

_____

_____

_____

¡A escuchar!

4-15 Depende del tiempo. Say which activity from each pair you and your friends are going to do according to the weather prediction you hear. As you hear the correct answer, listen, repeat, and place an **X** in the blank next to the selected activity.

MODELO   You see: _____ jugar al tenis en el parque   _____ estudiar en la biblioteca
              You hear: Esta tarde va a llover.
              You answer: **Vamos a estudiar en la biblioteca.**
              You hear: Vamos a estudiar en la biblioteca.
              You repeat: **Vamos a estudiar en la biblioteca.**
              You indicate: _____ jugar al tenis en el parque   **X** estudiar en la biblioteca

1. _____ esquiar en la montaña   _____ hacer esquí acuático en el lago

2. _____ tomar el sol en la playa   _____ pasar la tarde en casa

3. _____ jugar al fútbol americano   _____ hacer esquí acuático

4. _____ comer en el patio   _____ comer en el comedor

5. _____ ir al lago   _____ esquiar en la montaña

4-16 ¿Adónde vas? As a friend asks you where you are going, answer with the indicated place. Then when you are asked what you are going to do, answer with the logical activity from the list that follows. As you hear a verification of what you said, write the letter of the activity in the blank.

MODELO   You see: _____ a la piscina
              You hear: ¿Adónde vas?
              You answer: **Voy a la piscina.**
              You hear: ¿Qué vas a hacer?
              You answer: **Voy a nadar.**
              You hear: ¿Vas a nadar en la piscina?
              You indicate: **g** a la piscina

1. _____ al teatro   4. _____ a la montaña   7. _____ al gimnasio

2. _____ al cine   5. _____ al lago   8. _____ al estadio

3. _____ al museo   6. _____ al café   9. _____ al parque

a. ver una exposición de arte impresionista   g. nadar
b. pasear al perro   h. ver una obra
c. tomar una copa con los amigos   i. ver una película de aventuras
d. preparar la comida   j. hacer esquí acuático
e. ver un partido de fútbol   k. esquiar
f. levantar pesas

Tema 3 ¿Qué quieres hacer? ¿Puedes...?

4-17 ¿Quién? What does this woman say that she generally does on Fridays? Complete the sentences with the correct form of the verb from each list. Use the **yo** form of the verb if no other subject is stated in the sentence.

empezar	repetir	perder	dormir	encontrar	querer	poder

Siempre (1) _____ la misma rutina los viernes,

pero nunca (2) _____ esa rutina aburrida. No

(3) _____ hasta tarde porque

(4) _____ a trabajar a las siete y media de la

mañana. Generalmente (5) _____ dormir más

pero no (6) _____ porque si no salgo de la casa a

las siete, (7) _____ el autobús.

preferir	almorzar	contar	tener	servir	pedir

Mi novio y yo casi siempre (8) _____ juntos en

un restaurante cerca de mi trabajo que (9) _____

muy buena comida. Generalmente (nosotros)

(10) _____ un café después de comer. Mi novio

(11) _____ el café descafeinado porque trabaja

de noche los viernes y (12) _____ que dormir

por la tarde. Mi novio es muy divertido y siempre

(13) _____ muchos chistes (*jokes*).

volver	decir	jugar	venir

Después del trabajo, una amiga y yo (14) _____

al tenis. Ella siempre (15) _____ que juega mal

pero no es verdad. Ella gana más que yo. Después de jugar,

(16) _____ a casa generalmente. A veces, mi

amiga (17) _____ más tarde a mi casa a cenar.

4-18 ¿Qué quieren hacer? Complete the following sentences with the correct form of **ir** in the first blank and the correct form of **querer** followed by the logical activity from the list in the second.

correr	ver una exposición	hacer esquí acuático	tomar algo
trabajar	esquiar	cenar	ver una obra

MODELO Mis padres **van** al museo porque **quieren ver una exposición**.

1. Después de la exposición, mis padres _____ a un restaurante porque

   _____.

2. Mis amigos y yo _____ al lago mañana porque

   _____.

3. Mis abuelos _____ al teatro porque _____.

4. Mi prima _____ a la montaña para las vacaciones porque

   _____.

5. Esta tarde (yo) _____ al parque porque _____.

6. (Yo) No _____ a la oficina hoy porque no _____.

7. Ahora mi mejor amigo y yo _____ al café porque

   _____.

4-19 Una invitación. Two friends are making plans for this weekend. Complete their conversation by writing the correct form of the appropriate verb from those listed at the end of the line in each blank. The first one has been done as an example.

— ¿(1) _____**Puedes**_____ (tú) ir al cine conmigo este viernes? Hay una nueva película de

   aventuras que (yo) (2) _____ ver. (querer, poder)

— (Yo) No (3) _____ este viernes porque (yo)

   (4) _____ que trabajar. (tener, poder)

— (Nosotros) (5) _____ ir el sábado si (tú) (6) _____,

   o ¿(7) _____ (tú) que trabajar ese día también? (preferir, poder, tener)

— Sí, (yo) (8) _____ salir el sábado, pero la verdad es que (yo)

   (9) _____ ir a ver la obra de teatro en la universidad. (poder, preferir)

4-20 Hay mucho que hacer. Complete this paragraph about the rigors of school life by translating the verb in parentheses and using it in the correct form.

Mis compañeros de clase y yo (1) _____ (*sleep*) tres o cuatro horas por noche.

Nosotros (2) _____ (*prefer*) descansar más, pero no es posible. Todos nuestros

profesores (3) _____ (*think*) que tenemos mucho tiempo libre, pero no es cierto.

Algunos días yo no (4) _____ (*eat lunch*) porque no tengo tiempo. Yo no

(5) _____ (*find*) bastantes horas en el día. Mis amigos siempre

(6) _____ (*play*) al tenis los domingos, y (yo) (7) _____

(*want*) participar, pero no (8) _____ (*can, be able*). Mis padres siempre

(9) _____ (*say*) que es importante descansar, pero yo

(10) _____ (*think*) que ahora es más importante estudiar. Pobre de mí, nadie

(11) _____ (*understand*) mi problema. Creo que los profesores

(12) _____ (*can, be able*) dar (*give*) menos tarea, pero parece que ellos

(13) _____ (*prefer*) dar tanta (*so much*) tarea que los estudiantes no

(14) _____ (*can, be able*) hacerla (*do it*) toda.

4-21 Diario. Using **4-19 Una invitación** as an example, write a conversation in which your best friend invites you to do something that he/she often wants to do with you. Imagine that the invitation is for a time when you have to do something else, and explain why you cannot. Then discuss and decide on a time when you can do something together. If necessary, make contingency plans to do something else if the weather is bad. Use dialog dashes (—) to indicate a change of speaker, as in the **modelo**.

MODELO   — **¿Quieres jugar al tenis conmigo en el parque este sábado por la tarde?**
          — **No puedo este sábado porque tengo que ir a la casa de mis abuelos...**
          — **¿Prefieres...?**

_____

_____

_____

_____

_____

_____

¡A escuchar!

4-22 ¿Respuestas? Answer each question you hear with the logical response from each pair and place an **X** next to it. Then listen and repeat, as you hear the correct answer.

MODELO   You see: _____ a las siete y media   _____ hasta las siete y media

             You hear: Los lunes, ¿hasta qué hora duermes?

             You answer: **Los lunes, duermo hasta las siete y media.**

             You indicate: _____ a las siete y media   __X__ hasta las siete y media

             You hear: Los lunes, duermo hasta las siete y media.

             You repeat: **Los lunes, duermo hasta las siete y media.**

1. _____ a las nueve de la mañana   _____ hasta las nueve de la mañana

2. _____ a la cafetería de la universidad   _____ en la cafetería de la universidad

3. _____ a un café   _____ en un café

4. _____ a un café   _____ en un café

5. _____ a las seis y media   _____ hasta las seis y media

4-23 Una invitación. Listen to a conversation in which someone is making plans with his girlfriend on the phone. Then pause the recording and complete the following sentences according to what they say.

1. Esta noche él quiere asistir a _____ del grupo *Los Lobos,* pero ella no

   _____ porque tiene que acompañar a sus padres a

   _____ .

2. Mañana por la tarde, él quiere _____ , pero ella no puede porque

   _____ trabajar.

3. Ella _____ salir mañana por la noche porque

   _____ del trabajo a las seis.

4. Ella prefiere comer en un restaurante de _____ y

   después van a ir a _____ .

4-24 Entrevista. Using a complete sentence, answer each question you hear that a friend might ask you.

1. _____

2. _____

3. _____

4. _____

Tema 4 ¿Qué están haciendo ahora?

4-25 Una fiesta. Say what the indicated people are doing at this party by completing the sentences with the logical verb in the present progressive form.

Modelo   (Ellas) **Están preparando** la mesa.

1. (Ellos) _____ música.

2. (Ellas) _____ con sus novios.

3. (Ellos) _____ el partido de voléibol.

4. (Ella) _____ de su trabajo con un hombre que le gusta mucho.

5. (Él) _____ a una mujer aburrida hablar de su trabajo.

6. (Ellos) _____ un refresco (*a soft drink*).

7. (Ellos) _____ al voléibol.

8. (Él) _____ un chiste.

4-26 ¿Quién? Pick the appropriate subject in parentheses and write a sentence that describes the party in the illustration in the preceding activity. Remember to use the present progressive.

Modelo   (tres personas, nadie) dormir
Nadie está durmiendo.

1. (muchos invitados, nadie) comer pastel con helado

_____

2. (una mujer, dos mujeres) poner la mesa

_____

3. (varias personas, nadie) jugar en la piscina

_____

4. (alguien, nadie) sacar una foto

_____

5. (casi todos, casi nadie) hacer algo

_____

6. (unas personas, nadie) tomar el sol

_____

4-27 ¿Qué están haciendo? Explain what the pictured people are doing, using the present progressive.

MODELO   (Él) **Está viendo una exposición.**

1. (Yo) _____.

2. Mi amigo _____.

3. ¿(Ustedes) _____?

4. Mi hermano _____.

5. (Nosotros) _____.

6. (Yo) _____.

7. ¿(Tú) _____?

4-28 Diario. Imagine that you are at a party with people you know and you have called another friend on your cell phone to persuade him/her to join you. Write an imaginary conversation describing what the party is like and what people are doing at the moment. Think of real friends and what they usually are doing when you see them at parties, or else imagine new friends. Use dialogue dashes as in the **modelo** to indicate a change of speaker.

MODELO   — ¿Aló, Daniel? Habla Marco.
         — Hola Marco. ¿Qué estás haciendo? ¿Dónde estás? Oigo música...

_____

_____

_____

_____

_____

_____

_____

_____

_____

_____

_____

_____

_____

¡A escuchar!

4-29 ¿Qué están haciendo? You will hear questions about what different people are doing in the indicated locations. Answer with the logical activity from the list on the next page. Listen again and repeat as you hear the correct answer, and write the letter corresponding to the activity in the blank.

MODELO   You see: _____ en el centro comercial
         You hear: ¿Dónde está tu hermano?
         You answer: **Está comprando ropa en el centro comercial.**
         You hear: Está comprando ropa en el centro comercial.
         You repeat: **Está comprando ropa en el centro comercial.**
         You indicate: __f__ en el centro comercial

1. _____ en el lago

2. _____ en la biblioteca

3. _____ en un restaurante

4. _____ en su cama

5. _____ en el teatro

6. _____ en el gimnasio

7. _____ en el parque

8. _____ en la oficina

a. Está durmiendo.
b. Están viendo una obra.
c. Están haciendo su tarea.
d. Están cenando.
e. Está haciendo ejercicio y levantando pesas.
f. Está comprando ropa.
g. Está trabajando.
h. Está paseando al perro.
i. Está haciendo esquí acuático y tomando el sol.

4-30 ¿Quién es? Listen and repeat each statement you hear about what different people are doing and write the number of the statement next to the corresponding illustration.

a. _____   b. _____   c. _____

d. _____   e. _____

Now listen to the statements again and complete the following sentences.

1. Mi compañera de cuarto y yo _____.

2. Mi amigo _____ porque _____ a Italia.

3. Mi padre _____ solo _____.

4. Mi sobrino _____.

5. Mi compañera de clase _____ *La Bamba* con _____.

Tema 5 ¿Quieres ir al café?

4-31 En el café. Some people are ordering at a café. Complete each sentence with the logical word from the list.

jamón	café	jugo	helado	cerveza	té	vino	vainilla	bocadillo	agua	chocolate

1. Quiero una copa de _____ tinto, por favor.

2. Voy a tomar una _____. ¿Tienen *Corona*?

3. Me gustaría tomar un _____ mineral sin hielo, por favor.

4. Para mí, un _____ de naranja, por favor.

5. ¿Tienen _____ descafeinado?

6. Para los niños (*children*), un _____ caliente.

7. ¿Prefiere Ud. un _____ helado o caliente?

8. Quiero un _____ de _____ y queso.

9. ¿Prefieren _____ de chocolate o de _____?

4-32 ¿Hambre o sed? Say that the following people want the pictured items and whether they are hungry or thirsty.

MODELO   Yo **quiero un trozo de pastel**, por favor. **Tengo hambre.**

1.   2.   3.   4.   5.

1. ¿(Tú) _____? ¿_____?

2. (Yo) _____, por favor. _____.

3 (Nosotros) _____, por favor. _____.

4. Los niños _____.

5. Nadie _____. Nadie _____.

Capítulo 4 • En los ratos libres   **83**

4-33 ¿Qué quiere? Your friend will only have one of the items pictured in the preceding activity. To determine which one it is, answer the following three questions using the negative antonyms of the italicized words, and eliminate the appropriate items. Then complete the sentence saying what he prefers.

1. ¿Quiere *algo* con azúcar? _____

2. ¿Quiere queso *o* jamón? _____

3. ¿Toma cafeína *a veces*? _____

Mi amigo prefiere _____.

4-34 Expresiones negativas. You are taking care of a child who says no to everything. Answer each question as the child would, using the negative antonym of the italicized word.

MODELO   ¿Quieres comer *algo*?
          No, no quiero comer nada.

1. ¿Quieres tomar agua mineral *o* limonada?

_____

2. ¿Quieres chocolate con tu helado *también*?

_____

3. ¿Juegas con *algunos* amigos del barrio?

_____

4. ¿Viene *alguien* esta tarde a jugar contigo?

_____

5. ¿Duermes una siesta por la tarde *a veces*?

_____

4-35 Entrevista. Complete the following questions another student might ask you with words from the list. Then answer each one with a complete sentence in Spanish. Use each word only once.

alguien	algunos	ninguna	ni	algo	nadie

1. ¿Te gusta tomar _____ con los amigos en un café después de clase a veces?

_____

2. ¿Qué días de la semana no tienes _____ clase, _____ tienes que trabajar?

_____

3. ¿Vas a salir con _____ este fin de semana?

_____

4. ¿No hablas por teléfono con _____ cuando te quedas en casa los fines de semana?

_____

5. ¿Vienen _____ amigos a tu casa con frecuencia?

_____

4-36 Diario. Describe a restaurant or café where you sometimes have lunch. Include the following information in your description. If you are not sure of part of the information, say what you believe is right (**Creo que...**). If you never have lunch at a restaurant, pick a restaurant and pretend that you do. Say...

- at what restaurant you eat lunch and what type of food they serve (Mexican, Italian, Chinese, traditional [**tradicional**], sandwiches, fast food [**comida rápida**], etc.).
- why you prefer that restaurant.
- at what time they open and close.
- at what time they start to serve lunch (**el almuerzo**) and what time you prefer to eat lunch.
- with whom you generally have lunch there.
- what you generally order to drink.
- how you find (**encontrar**) the service (**el servicio**) there.
- whether you sometimes return there to have dinner the same day.

_____

_____

_____

_____

_____

_____

_____

_____

_____

_____

¡A escuchar!

4-37 ¿Tienen hambre o tienen sed? Repeat each order you hear at a café and indicate with **a** or **b** whether the person ordering is hungry (**a. tiene hambre**) or thirsty (**b. tiene sed**).

MODELO   You hear: Quiero una limonada con mucho hielo, por favor.
          You repeat: **Quiero una limonada con mucho hielo, por favor.**
          You indicate: __b__ *for* **tiene sed.**

1. ____   2. ____   3. ____   4. ____   5. ____   6. ____   7. ____   8. ____

4-38 En el restaurante. Answer each question about what is happening at this restaurant, using one of the two options given. Then listen as you hear the correct answer and place an **X** next to the word from each pair that you selected.

MODELO   You see: ____ alguien ____ nadie
          You hear: ¿Está pidiendo alguien la comida?
          You answer: **Sí, alguien está pidiendo la comida.**
          You hear: Sí, alguien está pidiendo la comida.
          You indicate: __X__ alguien ____ nadie

1. ____ alguien   ____ nadie   5. ____ alguien   ____ nadie

2. ____ y   ____ ni... ni   6. ____ algunas   ____ ninguna

3. ____ alguien   ____ nadie   7. ____ alguien   ____ nadie

4. ____ algunas   ____ ninguna   8. ____ y   ____ ni... ni

¡Trato hecho!

4-39 En la red. Spending time at a café with friends is one of the favorite leisure activities in Hispanic countries. On the Internet, find the homepages for two cafés in Hispanic countries by going to a Spanish language search engine such as *Yahoo Mexico, Terra, EresMás, Telépolis,* or *Ya.com.* Do a search for the words *café horas abierto* or the strings *café al aire libre* or *café bar,* limiting the search to *(paginas) en español.* Answer the following questions in Spanish about each café, except the last one, which you should answer in English.

Café 1

¿Cómo se llama el café y dónde está?

_____

¿A qué hora empiezan a servir la comida y qué sirven?

_____

¿A qué hora cierran?

_____

In English, give two other pieces of information you understand from the Web page.

_____

_____

Café 2

¿Cómo se llama el café y dónde está?

_____

¿A qué hora empiezan a servir la comida y qué sirven?

_____

¿A qué hora cierran?

_____

In English, give two other pieces of information you understand from the Web page.

_____

_____

4-40 Composición. Write a composition in which you describe your typical week giving the following information. You may incorporate what you wrote in your **Diarios** as appropriate.

Say...

- how late you sleep each day.
- where you go each day, what you do there, and when you return home.
- where you have breakfast, lunch, and dinner.
- in which restaurant you like to eat and why.
- when you can go out with your friends and what you generally do together.
- what the weather is going to be like tomorrow and what you are going to do in the morning, afternoon, and evening.
- what you plan to do with your friends next weekend.

_____

_____

_____

_____

_____

_____

_____

_____

_____

_____

_____

_____

_____

_____

_____

_____

_____

5 De compras

Tema 1 ¿Qué haces los sábados?

5-1 Los sábados de Noemí. Look at the illustrations below and describe what Noemí does on Saturdays using the structures from the list below. Conjugate the verbs in the third person (**ella**).

encontrarse con los amigos en el centro   relajarse en casa por la tarde   despertarse a las diez
acostarse tarde   lavarse los dientes   levantarse a las diez y media
maquillarse para salir   ducharse por la mañana

1.    2.    3.    4.

5.    6.    7.    8.

1. _____

2. _____

3. _____

4 _____

5. _____

6. _____

7. _____

8. _____

5-2 Los días de clase y los sábados. Victoria mentions the activities that she and her friends do during the week and on Saturdays. Fill in each blank with the correct form of the logical verb in parentheses.

MODELO   Los días de clase yo **asisto a clase** pero los sábados **me relajo en casa por la tarde**.
(relajarse en casa por la tarde, asistir a clase)

1. Los días de clase yo _____ pero los sábados

_____. (levantarse tarde, levantarse temprano)

2. Los días de clase mis amigos y yo _____ pero los

sábados _____. (comer en la cafetería,
encontrarse en un restaurante en el centro)

3. Los días de clase yo _____ pero los sábados

_____. (maquillarse para salir, vestirse para

ir a clase)

4. Los días de clase mis amigos y yo _____ pero los

sábados _____. (escribir ensayos por la
tarde, irse a un concierto)

5-3 ¿Reflexivo o no reflexivo? Complete the following paragraph about Ricardo's Saturdays by selecting the reflexive/reciprocal or non-reflexive/non-reciprocal form of the verb in parentheses. Conjugate the verb as necessary.

Ricardo trabaja mucho durante la semana y los sábados (1) _____

(quedar / quedarse) generalmente en casa. Pero por la mañana, su perro Dante siempre lo

(2) _____ (despertar / despertarse) a las diez y Ricardo

(3) _____ (vestir / vestirse) para ir al parque con Dante. Ricardo y Dante

(4) _____ (divertir / divertirse) mucho juntos. Después de correr en el parque,

Ricardo (5) _____ (bañar / bañarse) a Dante y (6) _____

(sentar / sentarse) en la sala a leer el periódico. Por la tarde, Ricardo y sus amigos

(7) _____ (llamar / llamarse) por teléfono y hacen planes para el domingo.

Por la noche, cuando (8) _____ (sentir / sentirse) cansado,

(9) _____ (acostar / acostarse) a Dante en el sofá y él también

(10) _____ (acostar / acostarse) en su cama.

5-4 Rutinas distintas. Amelia works nights and has the opposite routine from her roommate Rosa. What does she say? Complete each sentence with the antonym of the verb in italics.

Modelo   Rosa *se acuesta* a las diez de la noche pero a esa hora yo **me levanto.**

1. Yo *duermo* por la mañana pero Rosa _____ a las siete.

2. Rosa *se va* a la universidad temprano por la mañana pero yo _____ en casa.

3. Yo _____ en casa por la tarde pero Rosa *trabaja* toda la tarde.

4. Rosa *se siente aburrida* en el trabajo pero yo _____ jugando a los videojuegos por la tarde.

5. Por la noche, Rosa *se queda* en casa pero yo _____ al trabajo.

5-5 Diario. Write two paragraphs describing the activities that you generally do on Saturdays. In the first paragraph talk about the activities that you do by yourself, and in the second paragraph discuss what you and your friends do together during the weekend. Use the verbs and phrases presented in **Tema 1** of your textbook. You can also incorporate previous vocabulary that you learned to talk about leisure activities.

_____

_____

_____

_____

_____

_____

_____

_____

_____

_____

_____

_____

_____

_____

¡A escuchar!

5-6 Entrevista. Listen to some questions a person is asking a classmate. Answer each question by supplying the logical words in the cues that you see. Then listen and repeat as you hear the correct answer, and write the missing words in the blanks.

MODELO   You see: No, no _____ tarde los sábados.
                   You hear: ¿Te despiertas tarde los sábados?
                   You answer: **No, no me despierto tarde los sábados.**
                   You hear: No, no me despierto tarde los sábados.
                   You repeat and write: No, no **me despierto** tarde los sábados.

1. Sí, _____ el pelo todas las mañanas.

2. No, no _____ a la universidad los sábados por la mañana.

3. Sí, mis amigos y yo _____ por teléfono los sábados por la tarde.

4. No, no _____ en casa por la noche.

5. No, mis amigos y yo _____ generalmente en un café.

6. No, no _____ temprano los sábados por la noche.

5-7 ¿Qué haces los sábados? Listen as a classmate talks about what he does on Saturdays. Indicate whether the statements are also true about what you do by marking either **a. cierto** or **b. falso.** Then pause the recording and write a sentence indicating that the statement is also true for you, or change the statement to make it true for you.

MODELO   You hear: Los sábados duermo hasta tarde.
                   You indicate: **a.** cierto   You write: **Duermo hasta tarde también.**
                   Or: **b.** falso   You write: **No duermo hasta tarde.**

1. a. cierto   b. falso _____

2. a. cierto   b. falso _____

3. a. cierto   b. falso _____

4. a. cierto   b. falso _____

5. a. cierto   b. falso _____

5-8 No es lógico. Change the order of the following activities so that they are more logical. You will then hear the correct answer. Listen and say it again.

MODELO   You hear: Me lavo los dientes y desayuno.
                   You say: **Desayuno y me lavo los dientes.**
                   You hear: Desayuno y me lavo los dientes.
                   You repeat: **Desayuno y me lavo los dientes.**

Nombre: _____ Fecha: _____

Tema 2 ¿Qué haces con los amigos y los seres queridos?

5-9 Novios. Alma and Rafael love each other very much, but Estela and Pedro are close to breaking up. Which couple does each of the following things?

MODELO   llevarse mal
Estela y Pedro se llevan mal.

1. llevarse bien: _____.

2. verse casi todos los días: _____.

3. enojarse todos los sábados: _____.

4. besarse antes de despedirse: _____.

5. pelearse con frecuencia: _____.

6. ir a casarse algún día: _____.

7 encontrarse en un café después del trabajo: _____

_____.

8. no hablarse mucho: _____

_____.

9. comunicarse por correo electrónico a menudo (*often*): _____

_____.

5-10 ¿Qué hacen cuando...? Complete the following sentences with the logical expression of the two provided in parentheses. Conjugate the verb as necessary.

1. Cuando mi hermana y yo nos encontramos, generalmente _____.
   (despedirse / abrazarse)

2. Marta y Luis están enojados y no _____. (hablarse / separarse hasta tarde)

3. Mis padres y yo nos peleamos a veces, pero siempre _____.
   (reconciliarse / presentarse)

4. Cuando Antonio y su profesor se ven, _____. (casarse / darse la mano)

5. Alma y su madre se quieren mucho, pero a veces _____.
   (llevarse bien / pelearse)

6. Generalmente, mis amigos y yo _____. (encontrarse en un café / no hablarse por teléfono)

Capítulo 5 • De compras   **93**

5-11 ¿Qué van a hacer las amigas? Paloma, who has to work all weekend, is talking to her roommate, who doesn't have to work. What does Paloma say about herself and what does she say to her roommate? Write sentences with **tú** or **yo** as the subject.

MODELO   poder / despertarse tarde este sábado
               Tú puedes despertarte tarde este sábado.

1. tener que / levantarse temprano el sábado

   _____

2. no poder / relajarse

   _____

3. poder / quedarse en casa toda la mañana

   _____

4. tener que / irse temprano

   _____

5. ir a / divertirse con los amigos

   _____

6. ir a / sentirse muy triste en el trabajo

   _____

5-12 ¿Qué están haciendo? Complete the following sentences with the present progressive. Remember that the reflexive pronoun can be placed either before the conjugated form of **estar** or attached to the end of the present participle.

1. Mi padre se acaba de levantar y ahora _____ (ducharse) antes de ir a trabajar.

2. Ángel se acaba de bañar y ahora _____ (vestirse) para salir.

3. Raquel acaba de reconciliarse con su novio y _____ (besarse).

4. Laura y Miguel acaban de verse por primera vez y _____ (pedirse) los números de teléfono.

5. Lola y su compañera de casa generalmente se llevan muy bien pero ahora _____ (pelearse).

5-13 Alma y Rafael. Look at the illustrations below and indicate what Alma and Rafael are doing at this particular moment. Use the present progressive (**estar** + *present participle*) of the reflexive/reciprocal verbs that appear on page 136 of your textbook.

1.   2.   3.   4.

1. _____.

2. _____.

3. _____.

4. _____.

5-14 Diario. Write a paragraph describing your relationship with your friends and loved ones. Do you get along well? With which member of your family do you get along the best? What type of activities do you usually do together? Where do you generally meet? What do you say when you see each other? Do you have a boyfriend or a girlfriend? Are you going to get married one day?

_____

_____

_____

_____

_____

_____

_____

_____

_____

_____

_____

_____

¡A escuchar!

5-15 Mi mejor amigo y yo. Listen to the following questions and indicate whether they are true or false for you.

MODELO   You hear: ¿Se hablan por teléfono tu mejor amigo y tú todos los días?
    You write: **Sí, mi mejor amigo y yo nos hablamos por teléfono todos los días.** *or*
    No, mi mejor amigo y yo nunca nos hablamos por teléfono. *or*
    Mi mejor amigo y yo nos hablamos por teléfono con frecuencia.

1. _____

2. _____

3. _____

4. _____

5. _____

6. _____

7. _____

5-16 El Club Trapecio. Listen to the following phone conversation between Estrella and Carlos and fill in the blanks with the verbs that you hear.

— Hola, Carlos. Soy Estrella.

— Hola, Estrella. ¿Cómo estás?

— Bien, gracias. Oye, Carlos, ¿(1) _____
con el grupo esta noche a las once en El Club Trapecio?

— No, no puedo. Esta noche (2) _____ a las diez.

—¿Te sientes mal?

— No, pero mañana por la mañana (3) _____
temprano para un examen de química.

— Claro, y (4) _____ en casa esta noche. Lo entiendo.

— Gracias de todos modos (*anyway*). ¿(5) _____
el sábado por la tarde para ver una película?

— Sí, Carlos, y (6) _____ mucho contigo también.

— Muy bien, hasta el sábado.

Tema 3 ¿Qué te vas a poner?

5-17 De moda. Look at the illustrations below and name the different pieces of clothing and accessories for women and men shown in the drawings. Be sure to use the correct form of *a(n)* (**un, una**) or *some* (**unos, unas**).

1. _____

2. _____

3. _____

4. _____

5. _____

6. _____

7. _____

8. _____

9. _____

10. _____

11. _____

12. _____

5-18 Ropa para cada ocasión. Decide what is the most appropriate piece of clothing for each occasion.

1. En la playa llevo _____ y sandalias.

2. Para hacer ejercicio, uso _____, camiseta y pantalones cortos.

3. Cuando voy a una entrevista de trabajo (*job interview*) me pongo un _____,

4. Cuando está nevando llevo un abrigo y _____.

5. Cuando llueve me pongo un _____ y un sombrero.

6. Siempre llevo _____ con mis zapatos.

5-19 ¿Éste o ése? The following shoppers like what they are trying on more than the other item being considered. Write the demonstrative adjective or pronoun in the correct form in the logical blank. Use the pronouns with an accent if the noun has been left out.

MODELO   **Esa** falda es fea. Me gusta más **ésta**. (este/éste, ese/ése)

1. Voy a comprar _____ zapatos porque _____ son muy caros. (este/éste, aquel/aquél)

2. No me gusta mucho _____ corbata. Prefiero _____. (este/éste, ese/ése)

3. Me gusta _____ suéter más que _____. (este/éste, aquel/aquél)

4. Voy a comprar _____ botas porque _____ no son de mi número (*size*). (este/éste, ese/ése)

5. No me gusta _____ camiseta de rayas. Prefiero

_____ de un solo color. (este/éste, aquel/aquél)

5-20 ¡Qué caro! Imagine that the person who is trying on clothes in the illustration below is making comments about the prices and styles of the clothes. Complete the following sentences with the appropriate demonstrative adjective or pronoun for each situation, from her point of view.

MODELO   Me gusta **este** vestido largo, pero es muy caro.

1. _____ zapatos son muy bonitos, pero también son más caros; cuestan ochenta y nueve dólares.

2. _____ vestido corto es más barato que _____. ¿Cuál te gusta más?

3. Necesito una blusa blanca; _____ no es muy cara.

4. _____ sombrero no me gusta. Voy a comprar

   _____; sólo cuesta treinta y cinco dólares.

5. Me gusta _____ falda, pero no necesito una falda ahora; busco un vestido.

6. ¿Prefieres _____ zapatos de setenta dólares o

   _____ de sesenta y cinco?

5-21 Intérprete. Julia is shopping with her friend Rita, who doesn't speak Spanish. Translate Rita's comments below.

1. *She needs a silk blouse and a wool skirt.*

   _____

2. *No, she doesn't like this black skirt; she prefers that gray skirt.*

   _____

3. *Yes, this blue blouse is perfect.*

   _____

4. *No, she doesn't like those blue shoes; she likes those pink shoes over there.*

   _____

5-22 Diario. Write a paragraph describing the clothes that you and your professors generally wear to class. Also describe what you wear to play sports and to go out with friends on the weekend.

_____

_____

_____

_____

_____

¡A escuchar!

5-23 ¿Lógico o ilógico? You will hear some statements about clothing. Mark **lógico** if the statement makes sense, **ilógico** if it does not.

MODELO   You hear: Cuando voy a una boda llevo corbata y camiseta.
          You mark: _____ lógico   __X__ ilógico

1. _____ lógico _____ ilógico   5. _____ lógico _____ ilógico

2. _____ lógico _____ ilógico   6. _____ lógico _____ ilógico

3. _____ lógico _____ ilógico   7. _____ lógico _____ ilógico

4. _____ lógico _____ ilógico   8. _____ lógico _____ ilógico

5-24 ¿Cuál prefieres? You are shopping with Raúl. He shows you several items and asks if you like each one. In each case, indicate that you prefer the one that is on the counter. Mark your answers below.

MODELO   You hear: ¿Te gusta este traje?
          You mark: **No. Prefiero ése.**

1. _____ No, prefiero ése. _____ No, prefiero ésos. _____ No, prefiero ésa. _____ No, prefiero ésas.

2. _____ No, prefiero ése. _____ No, prefiero ésos. _____ No, prefiero ésa. _____ No, prefiero ésas.

3. _____ No, prefiero ése. _____ No, prefiero ésos. _____ No, prefiero ésa. _____ No, prefiero ésas.

4. _____ No, prefiero ése. _____ No, prefiero ésos. _____ No, prefiero ésa. _____ No, prefiero ésas.

5. _____ No, prefiero ése. _____ No, prefiero ésos. _____ No, prefiero ésa. _____ No, prefiero ésas.

5-25 Entrevista. Listen to some questions a person is asking a classmate. Answer each question by supplying the logical words in the cues that you see. Then listen and repeat as you hear the correct answer, and write the missing words in the blanks.

MODELO   You see: No, no me pongo _____ para ir a la oficina.
          You hear: ¿Te pones vaqueros para ir a trabajar?
          You answer: **No, no me pongo vaqueros para ir a la oficina.**
          You hear: No, no me pongo vaqueros para ir a la oficina.
          You repeat and write: No, no me pongo **vaqueros** para ir a la oficina.

1. Sí, me pongo un _____ para salir por la noche.

2. No, no me pongo un _____ cuando hace calor.

3. Sí, llevo _____ cuando voy a la playa.

4. Sí, siempre uso _____ para correr en el parque.

5. No, no llevo _____ cuando hace frío.

Tema 4 ¿Cuánto cuesta?

5-26 En el escaparate (*window*). Name the items in the illustration below that are found in a store.

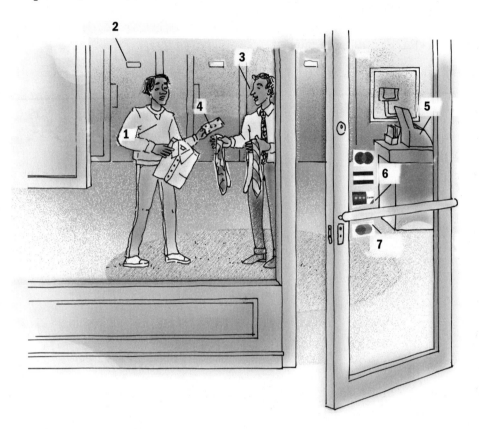

1. _____   5. _____

2. _____   6. _____

3. _____   7. _____

4. _____

5-27 ¿A qué se refiere? Which of the customer's statements goes with each of the salesclerk's statements? Write its letter in the blank.

<table>
<tr><td align="center">**El dependiente**</td><td align="center">**El cliente**</td></tr>
<tr><td>1. _____ No, no la tengo mayor.</td><td>a. ¿Los tiene más baratos?</td></tr>
<tr><td>2. _____ Tengo unos zapatos de 80 dólares.</td><td>b. ¿Tiene una talla más grande?</td></tr>
<tr><td>3. _____ ¿Le gusta este traje gris?</td><td>c. Busco un suéter.</td></tr>
<tr><td>4. _____ ¿Cómo lo quiere, de lana o de algodón?</td><td>d. Me las voy a llevar.</td></tr>
<tr><td>5. _____ Estas sandalias son muy bonitas y muy razonables.</td><td>e. Sí, ¿me lo puedo probar?</td></tr>
</table>

5-28 ¿En qué puedo servirle? You are out shopping for a new T-shirt and pants. Complete the conversation you have with the salesperson with the appropriate direct object pronoun.

Encargado: ¿Busca al dependiente?

Ud.: Sí, (1) _____ busco.

Dependiente: Aquí estoy, ¿en que puedo servirle?

Ud.: Busco una camiseta de algodón.

Dependiente: ¿Cómo (2) _____ quiere?

Ud.: (3) _____ quiero de algodón, pero no quiero gastar más de veinte dólares.

Dependiente: Tenemos unas camisetas de colores muy modernas y a buen precio.

Ud.: ¿(4) _____ tienen en azul o blanco?

Dependiente: Sí, claro, éstas en azul y blanco son muy razonables.

Ud.: Sí, ésta azul me gusta. Me (5) _____ voy a llevar.

Dependiente: ¿Necesita algo más?

Ud.: Sí, busco también unos pantalones.

Dependiente: Y, ¿cómo (6) _____ busca? ¿Vaqueros o de cuero?

Ud.: (7) _____ prefiero de cuero. Éstos me gustan, ¿tienen mi talla?

Dependiente: ¿Qué talla lleva usted?

Ud.: Llevo la talla 14.

Dependiente: Lo siento, no (8) _____ tenemos.

Ud.: Bueno, me llevo la camiseta sólo.

Dependiente: Y, ¿cómo (9) _____ va a pagar?

Ud.: Con tarjeta de crédito. ¿Aceptan tarjetas de crédito?

Dependiente: Sí, (10) _____ aceptamos todas.

5-29 ¿Te los vas a llevar? Answer the following questions by substituting the direct object with the appropriate pronoun.

MODELO   ¿Vas a comprar esos zapatos?
Sí, los voy a comprar. / Sí, voy a comprarlos.

1. ¿Aceptan tarjetas de crédito en todas las tiendas?

   No, no _____.

2. ¿Te vas a llevar este abrigo?

   Sí, _____.

3. ¿Usas mucho el impermeable?

   No, no _____.

4. ¿Te pones corbata para ir a trabajar?

   Sí, _____.

5. ¿Llevas siempre pantalones cortos para hacer ejercicio?

   Sí, generalmente _____.

6. ¿Vas a llevar una falda a la fiesta?

   No, no _____.

5-30 Diario. Write a paragraph comparing your shopping habits with those of your best friend. How often do you go shopping? Do you like to shop alone or with friends? Where do you like to go shopping? Do you always buy clothes on sale? How much money do you usually spend on clothes per month?

_____

_____

_____

_____

_____

_____

_____

_____

¡A escuchar!

5-31 No, nunca... Answer the following questions that another student might ask you with a complete sentence in Spanish.

MODELO   You hear: ¿Pagas con tarjeta de crédito a veces?
                    You write: **Sí, pago con tarjeta de crédito a veces.** *or*
                                      No, nunca pago con tarjeta de crédito.

1. _____

2. _____

3. _____

4. _____

5. _____

6. _____

5-32 En la zapatería. Listen to some exchanges between a male client and a salesperson. Answer each question by supplying the logical words in the cues that you see. Then listen and repeat as you hear the correct answer, and write the missing words in the blanks.

MODELO   You see: Sí, claro, _____ tenemos de lana.
                    You hear: ¿Tienen calcetines de lana?
                    You answer: **Sí, claro, los tenemos de lana.**
                    You hear: Sí, claro, los tenemos de lana.
                    You repeat and write: Sí, claro, **los** tenemos de lana.

1. Sí, _____ puedo ayudar.

2. No, no _____ tenemos en marrón, sólo en negro.

3. Sí, _____ tenemos más grande.

4. Sí, claro, _____ puede probar.

5. Sí, _____ tengo en negro.

6. Sí, _____ tengo.

7. Sí, _____ voy a llevar.

8. Sí, _____ aceptamos todas, de crédito y de débito.

Tema 5 ¿Para quién es?

5-33 ¿Adónde vas para...? Indicate where Macarena's family goes to buy the following things or run the following errands.

1. Mi madre va a _____ para comprar unos aretes para mi hermana.

2. Mi padre necesita pasar por _____ para probarse unos zapatos.

3. Mis hermanos tienen que ir a _____ para cortarse el pelo.

4. Mi abuelo quiere pasar por _____ para comprar unos pasteles para su nieto.

5. Yo voy a _____ para comprar un diccionario para mi clase de español.

5-34 No tienes mucho dinero. Sara is looking for a gift for her boyfriend Manuel, but she doesn't have much money. Complete her conversation with a friend using words from the list.

anillo	descuento	cadena	regalo	cartera	gorra

— Necesito comprar un (1) _____ para mi novio.

— ¿Qué le vas a comprar?

— No sé, me gustaría comprarle una (2) _____ de plata.

— Es un regalo un poco caro.

— Sí, también puedo comprarle una (3) _____ de cuero.

— Sí, o también una (4) _____. Es un regalo más razonable.

— Él va a comprar un (5) _____ de oro para mí, y quiero tener un regalo bueno para él.

— Mira (*Look*), en la joyería tienen un (6) _____ del 50 por ciento.

— Perfecto. Vamos a mirar las cadenas de plata.

5-35 ¿Por o para? Match each sentence's beginning with a logical ending with **por** or **para**. Write the letter of the logical ending in the blank.

1. _____ Es un juguete muy apropiado...   a. para probarme estos vaqueros.

2. _____ Generalmente no pago mucho...   b. para mis próximas vacaciones.

3. _____ Me gusta estudiar en la biblioteca...   c. para un niño de diez años.

4. _____ Necesito comprar un traje de baño...   d. por Internet.

5. _____ Busco los probadores...   e. por mi ropa.

6. _____ Me gusta comprar cosas...   f. por la semana.

7. _____ Esta tienda es muy famosa...   g. para pagar?

8. _____ ¿Adónde vamos...   h. por su ropa elegante.

5-36 Hola, Conchita, soy Paz. Complete the following conversation between two friends who are making plans for tonight with the appropriate preposition, **por** or **para**.

— Hola, Conchita, soy Paz.

— Hola, Paz, ¿cómo estás?

— Bien, te llamo (1) _____ invitarte al cine esta noche.

— Gracias (2) _____ la invitación. ¿Qué película vamos a ver?

— *Los otros*. Es una película famosa (3) _____ sus efectos especiales.

— Me parece muy bien.

— ¿A qué hora paso (4) _____ ti?

— A las ocho. Tengo que escribir un ensayo (5) _____ mi clase de psicología antes de salir.

— Perfecto, antes tengo que ir al centro (6) _____ hacer unos mandados.

— ¿Qué tienes que hacer?

— Tengo que pasar (7) _____ la librería (8) _____ comprar un libro

(9) _____ mi padre, y también necesito trabajar (10) _____ tres horas.

— Buena suerte y hasta las ocho.

— Hasta luego, Conchita.

5-37 Fragmentos. Marta gets an invitation from her friend Antonio to go out to dinner tonight. Form sentences with the following information, selecting **por** or **para**.

1. Marta / vestirse / por *o* para / salir a cenar con su amigo Antonio

   _____

2. Marta / estar / sorprendida / por *o* para / la invitación de Antonio

   _____

3. Marta y Antonio / hablarse / por *o* para / teléfono / por *o* para / decidir / adónde ir a cenar

   _____

4. Marta / conocer / un restaurante famoso / por *o* para / su pescado (*fish*)

   _____

5. Antonio / ir a hacer / una reserva / por *o* para / las siete y media

   _____

6. Antonio / ir a / pasar / por *o* para / Marta / a las siete

   _____

5-38 Diario. Write a paragraph describing the errands that you usually run during the week and on the weekends, and the places where you need to go to run these errands. Why do you like these stores? Are they in your neighborhood? Are they close to the university?

   _____

   _____

   _____

   _____

   _____

   _____

   _____

   _____

¡A escuchar!

5-39 ¿La carnicería o la pescadería? You will hear some statements about shopping. Repeat each statement and select the appropriate store in each case.

MODELO   You see: _____ a la zapatería   _____ a la peluquería
You hear: Me voy a cortar el pelo.
You repeat: **Me voy a cortar el pelo.**
You indicate: _____ a la zapatería   **X** a la peluquería

1. _____ a la carnicería   _____ a la pescadería   4. _____ a la carnicería   _____ a la joyería

2. _____ a la pastelería   _____ a la peluquería   5. _____ a la pastelería   _____ a la librería

3. _____ a la joyería   _____ a la zapatería   6. _____ a la pescadería   _____ a la librería

5-40 ¿Y tú? Answer the following questions a friend might ask you with a complete sentence in Spanish indicating whether they are true or false for you.

1. _____

2. _____

3. _____

4. _____

5. _____

6. _____

7. _____

8. _____

5-41 Desacuerdos. Listen to a conversation between a wife and her husband, María José and Alejandro, who don't agree on what they want to do this weekend. List the activities that María José wants to do under **María José quiere...**, and the activities that Alejandro wants to do under **Alejandro quiere....**

María José quiere...	**Alejandro quiere...**
_____	_____
_____	_____
_____	_____
_____	_____

¡Trato hecho!

5-42 En la red. Search for famous department stores in some Hispanic countries, such as *El Corte Inglés* in Spain or *Sanborn's* in Mexico. You can extend your search by entering *Department stores in Latin America.* Check the sites you find for the information requested below and answer the questions in English. Write down the addresses of the interesting and useful sites you discover and share them with your instructor and other students.

Addresses of useful and interesting sites:

www._____

www._____

www._____

1. What are the different departments in the stores?

   _____

   _____

   _____

2. Name at least ten items that you can buy in the clothing department or fashion section.

   _____

   _____

3. What do you think some of the best selling items might be?

   _____

   _____

4. Compare the sites from the Spanish department stores to an American department store site.

   _____

   _____

   _____

   _____

Capítulo 5 • De compras   **109**

5-43 Composición. Using what you have learned in this chapter, write a composition describing your shopping habits and those of your family. What stores do you and your family frequent and what types of things do you buy there? How much money do you and your family spend on clothes, on dining out, or on entertainment?

_____

_____

_____

_____

_____

_____

_____

_____

_____

_____

_____

_____

_____

_____

_____

_____

_____

_____

6   De viaje

Tema 1 ¿Adónde fuiste de vacaciones?

6-1 Descanso de primavera. A student who spent spring break in New York City is talking to a classmate who went to Cancún about what they did on their trips. Which of the following things would he say he did in New York and which would he ask if his friend did in Cancún? Write sentences in the **yo** form or questions in the **tú** form under the appropriate heading. Two have already been done as examples.

visitar la Estatua de la Libertad
ver tres obras de teatro
nadar mucho
hablar sólo en español
probar la comida del Yucatán
tomar el metro (*subway*) más que el autobús
ir a la playa todos los días
correr cada mañana en el Parque Central

tomar el sol todo el tiempo
ir a varios museos
salir en velero
pescar en el mar
visitar las ruinas mayas cerca de allí
alojarse en un hotel cerca de la playa
asistir a un partido de los *Knicks*

En Nueva York, yo...   **Visité la Estatua de la Libertad.**

_____

_____

_____

_____

_____

_____

En Cancún, ¿tú...?   **¿Nadaste mucho?**

_____

_____

_____

_____

_____

Capítulo 6 • De viaje   **111**

6-2 Un turista enfermo. During his vacation, Oswaldo fell ill and had to spend the day at the hotel while his friends went out on the town. Write sentences saying who did each of the following things.

MODELO   levantarse temprano para salir / sólo levantarse para comer
           Sus amigos se levantaron temprano para salir, pero Oswaldo sólo se levantó para comer.

1. pasar un día estupendo / pasar un día muy aburrido

    _____

2. tomar un taxi al centro / tomar antibióticos

    _____

3. ver muchos sitios históricos / ver la tele todo el día

    _____

4. comer en su cuarto / comer en un restaurante famoso

    _____

5. quedarse en el hotel todo el día / quedarse en el centro hasta la medianoche

    _____

6-3 Por última vez. Complete the following questions a friend might ask you with the appropriate form of the preterite. Then answer each question saying when the indicated people did the named activity.

hoy   ayer   anteayer   hace... días (semanas, meses)   nunca
el sábado (mes, año) pasado   la semana pasada   hace mucho tiempo

MODELO   ¿Cuándo fue la última vez que alguien de otra ciudad te **visitó** (visitar)?
           Mis primos de Santa Fe me vistaron el mes pasado.

1. ¿Cuándo fue la última vez que tu mejor amigo te _____ (invitar) a hacer algo?

    _____

2. ¿Cuándo fue la última vez que tus padres te _____ (llevar) de vacaciones?

    _____

3. ¿Cuándo fue la última vez que _____ (acampar, tú)?

    _____

4. ¿Cuándo fue la última vez que _____ (viajar, tú) en avión (*by plane*)?

    _____

Nombre: _____ Fecha: _____

6-4 ¿Qué tal las vacaciones? Two students are talking about one's vacation in Spain. Write the correct preterite forms of the verbs in parentheses in the logical blanks. The first statement has been done as an example.

— ¿**Te quedaste** (tú) aquí durante las vacaciones o **saliste** (tú) de viaje? (salir, quedarse)

— (Yo) (1) _____ una semana en Sevilla, España, y me

   (2) _____ mucho. (pasar, gustar)

— No (3) _____ sola, ¿verdad? Adela te (4) _____,
   ¿no? (viajar, acompañar *to accompany*)

— No, no (5) _____ Adela. Mi hermana (6) _____
   conmigo. (ir, ser)

— ¿(7) _____ (Uds.) otras ciudades o (8) _____
   (Uds.) toda la semana en Sevilla? (pasar, visitar)

— No, también (9) _____ (nosotras) a Granada, donde

   (10) _____ (nosotras) la Alhambra. (ver, ir)

— ¿(11) _____ (tú) muchas fotos? (12) _____ (yo)
   que ese palacio es muy bonito. (leer, sacar)

— Mi hermana (13) _____ varias fotos y yo (14) _____
   unas tarjetas postales. (sacar, comprar)

— ¿Cuándo (15) _____ (Uds.)? ¿(16) _____ (Uds.)
   anoche? (regresar, llegar)

— No, (nosotras) (17) _____ esta mañana y (yo) sólo

   (18) _____ dos horas antes de venir a clase. Por eso, estoy muy cansada.
   (descansar, llegar)

6-5 Diario. Write a paragraph describing the last time you went away for the weekend. Tell where you went, where you stayed, and several things that you and those with you did.

_____

_____

_____

_____

_____

© 2006 Pearson Education, Inc.   **Capítulo 6** • De viaje   **113**

¡A escuchar!

6-6 ¿Adónde fueron? You will hear someone make statements about what he and others he knows did on their vacation. Repeat what he says, adding a statement explaining to which place from each pair they went, as in the **modelo**. Then listen and repeat as you hear the correct answer and place an **X** next to the place that is stated.

MODELO
You see: _____ al campo _____ al mercado
You hear: Mis amigos y yo acampamos y descendimos por el río en canoa.
You say: **Mis amigos y yo fuimos al campo donde acampamos y descendimos por el río en canoa.**
You hear: Mis amigos y yo fuimos al campo donde acampamos y descendimos por el río en canoa.
You repeat: **Mis amigos y yo fuimos al campo donde acampamos y descendimos por el río en canoa.**
You indicate: __X__ al campo _____ al mercado

1. _____ a Europa _____ a Sudamérica

2. _____ al mar _____ a la montaña

3. _____ al río _____ a la Ciudad de México

4. _____ a la playa _____ a un sitio histórico

5. _____ al mercado _____ a varios restaurantes

6. _____ al mercado _____ al museo

7. _____ al mercado _____ al lago

8. _____ al bosque _____ a un parque de atracciones

6-7 ¿Qué hicieron? Listen to a conversation in which two friends discuss their vacations and complete the following sentences according to what you hear.

Miranda (1) _____ unas vacaciones muy

(2) _____ en México. (3) _____ a sus

(4) _____ en Guadalajara y luego (5) _____ a

Acapulco. Le (6) _____ mucho las playas de Acapulco. Enrique

(7) _____ unas vacaciones muy (8) _____. Sus amigos

y él no (9) _____ a acampar porque (10) _____ toda

la semana. Enrique (11) _____ en casa y vio

(12) _____ en estas vacaciones.

Tema 2 ¿Qué tal el vuelo?

6-8 Un vuelo. Describe this passenger's flight. Did she do the listed things **antes de despegar, durante el vuelo,** or **después de aterrizar**? Write sentences placing each item from the list in the logical order with the verbs in the **ella** form of the preterite. The first one has been done as an example.

llegar al aeropuerto dos horas antes del vuelo   abrocharse el cinturón de seguridad
leer la revista de la aerolínea   salir del aeropuerto
facturar su equipaje   buscar un taxi
ir a la sala de espera   subir al taxi
bajar del avión   hablar con el pasajero al lado de ella
recoger su equipaje   ver toda la ciudad por la ventanilla
esperar una hora y media   almorzar en el avión
subir al avión   ir a su hotel

Antes de despegar   **Llegó al aeropuerto dos horas antes del vuelo.**

_____

_____

_____

_____

_____

Durante el vuelo   _____

_____

_____

_____

_____

Después de aterrizar   _____

_____

_____

_____

_____

Capítulo 6 • De viaje   **115**

6-9 ¿En qué orden? In what order did the following things happen before or during a flight? Write logical sentences using the subjects indicated in parentheses.

MODELO   (yo) pagar el pasaje de avión en la agencia de viajes / sacar dinero del banco
            Saqué dinero del banco y pagué el pasaje de avión en la agencia de viajes.

1. (el avión) despegar a las ocho de la mañana / aterrizar a las cuatro de la tarde

   _____

2. (el pasajero a mi lado) leer durante todo el vuelo / sacar un libro

   _____

3. (yo) sacar los audífonos (*earphones*) / oír música

   _____

4. (yo) bajar del avión / abrazar a mi amiga que me recogió en el aeropuerto / llegar a mi destino

   _____

6-10 Dos viajes. Petra is telling how she planned her vacation trip so well that everything went smoothly, but her roommate did not, and had a lot of problems. Complete her comparison of each one's trip with the pronouns **yo** or **ella** and the preterite forms of the indicated verbs.

MODELO   empezar: **Yo empecé** a hacer preparativos (*preparations*) dos meses antes del viaje,
            pero **ella empezó** en el último momento.

1. buscar: _____ un hotel después de llegar, pero

   _____ un hotel por Internet antes de salir.

2. pagar: _____ mucho por su pasaje de avión porque esperó hasta el último

   momento para comprarlo, pero _____ muy poco porque compré el mío
   (*mine*) con dos meses de antelación.

3. llegar: _____ muy bien a mi destino, pero _____
   muy cansada.

4. leer: _____ mi guía para hacer un itinerario antes de salir, pero

   _____ nunca _____ su guía.

5. sacar: _____ fotos con una cámara desechable (*disposable*) porque dejó su

   cámara en casa, pero _____ fotos con mi nueva cámara digital que compré
   para el viaje.

6-11 La última lección de español. Complete the following questions another student might ask you about your most recent Spanish class with the indicated forms of the verbs. Then answer each question truthfully.

1. ¿_____ (llegar, tú) tarde o a tiempo (*on time*) a clase?

   _____

2. ¿_____ (oír, Uds.) un ejercicio del CD de español en clase?

   _____

3. ¿_____ (leer, Uds.) la lectura *Operación salida* en la página 184?

   _____

4. ¿_____ (almorzar, tú) antes o después de clase?

   _____

5. ¿_____ (empezar, tú) la tarea inmediatamente después de clase?

   _____

6. ¿_____ (buscar, tú) algunas palabras en un diccionario para comprender la tarea?

   _____

6-12 Diario. Write a paragraph describing the last time you took a flight. Tell where you went, whether you arrived early or late at the airport, what you did before, during, and after the flight, and where you went after leaving the airport.

_____

_____

_____

_____

_____

_____

_____

_____

¡A escuchar!

6-13 Un vuelo. Answer each question you hear about a flight negatively, and explain why with the logical reason from each pair. Then listen and repeat as you hear the correct answer and indicate the reason with an **X**.

MODELO   You see: _____ Busqué el mejor precio.   _____ Lo compré en el último momento.
You hear: ¿Pagaste mucho por el pasaje de avión?
You say: **No, no pagué mucho por el pasaje de avión porque busqué el mejor precio.**
You hear: No, no pagué mucho por el pasaje de avión porque busqué el mejor precio.
You repeat: **No, no pagué mucho por el pasaje de avión porque busqué el mejor precio.**
You indicate: __X__ Busqué el mejor precio.   _____ Lo compré en el último momento.

1. _____ El avión salió con retraso (*delayed*).   _____ El avión salió a tiempo (*on time*).

2. _____ Tomé un vuelo directo.   _____ Tomé un vuelo con escalas.

3. _____ Me gustó mucho la comida.   _____ Almorcé antes de salir.

4. _____ Sólo llevé una maleta pequeña.   _____ Llevé tres maletas grandes.

5. _____ Me senté junto a la ventanilla.   _____ Me senté junto al pasillo.

6. _____ Me senté en la parte delantera (*front*).   _____ Me senté al fondo del avión.

7. _____ Llegamos a tiempo.   _____ Un pasajero aburrido me habló todo el tiempo.

8. _____ El taxi me llevó al hotel.   _____ Un amigo me recogió.

6-14 Un mal vuelo. Listen as Diego talks to his roommate about a bad flight. Then complete the following sentences by filling in the blanks with appropriate verbs in the preterite, according to what you hear in the dialogue.

1. El vuelo _____ a tiempo.

2. Veinte minutos después de despegar, los pasajeros _____ algo en uno de los

   motores y algunos _____ fuego (*fire*).

3. El avión empezó a volver al aeropuerto de donde _____.

4. Una pasajera a la derecha de Diego _____ a llorar (*to cry*), otra a su izquierda

   _____ tranquilamente y Diego _____ un poco.

5. El avión _____ al aeropuerto y _____ sin problema.

6. Diego _____ otro vuelo más tarde y por eso _____
   con retraso (*delayed*).

Nombre: _____ Fecha: _____

Tema 3 ¿Te gustó el hotel?

6-15 En el hotel. Complete the following paragraph describing a stay in a hotel with the names of the corresponding objects or persons from the illustrations.

Cuando llegué al hotel fui primero a _____**la recepción**_____. El

(1) _____ me ofreció una habitación en la planta baja al fondo del

(2) _____, pero la otra (3) _____ dijo que había (*there*

was) otra habitación disponible en el segundo piso. Otra (4) _____ del hotel me

recomendó tomar la habitación del segundo piso para tener buenas vistas al mar. Mis hijos subieron a la

habitación por la (5) _____, pero yo tomé el (6) _____.

Un (7) _____ me ayudó con nuestro (8) _____.

Cuando abrí la puerta con la (9) _____ encontramos una habitación muy bonita

con excelentes vistas al (10) _____ y salimos inmediatamente al

(11) _____. Esa noche mis hijos durmieron en la

(12) _____ y yo tuve que acostarme en el (13) _____.

Encontramos el (14) _____ pequeño pero había una bañera (*bathtub*) con

(15) _____ para ducharnos.

6-16 El fin de semana pasado. Felipe stayed home all weekend while his two housemates were out on the town. Write sentences saying whether Felipe or his roommates did the following things.

MODELOS   preferir quedarse en casa: **Felipe prefirió quedarse en casa.**
              preferir salir con los amigos: **Sus compañeros de casa prefirieron salir con los amigos.**

1. vestirse con ropa elegante para salir: _____.

2. limpiar la casa: _____.

3. ir a muchas fiestas: _____.

4. jugar con los videojuegos en casa: _____.

5. divertirse con los amigos: _____.

6. acostarse temprano el sábado: _____.

7. dormir mucho: _____.

8. no volver a casa el sábado: _____.

9. despertarse muy cansado(s) el lunes: _____.

6-17 ¡Yo también! Say whether you did each of the things listed in the preceding activity last weekend.

MODELOS   **No, no preferí quedarme en casa.**
              Sí, preferí salir con los amigos.

1. _____

2. _____

3. _____

4. _____

5. _____

6. _____

7. _____

8. _____

9. _____

6-18 Un día cargado. Describe this man's busy morning by putting each verb in parentheses in the logical blank, using the **él** form of the preterite.

MODELO   No **durmió** mucho porque **se divirtió** hasta tarde con los amigos la noche anterior. (divertirse, dormir)

1. _____ a las tres y _____ a las siete. (acostarse, despertarse)

2. _____, _____ y _____ para el trabajo. (salir, bañarse, vestirse)

3. _____ tarde a la oficina porque _____ el autobús. (perder, llegar)

4. Después de llegar, _____ un café, _____ en su escritorio y _____ a trabajar. (sentarse, empezar, servirse)

5. A mediodía _____ en un restaurante cerca de su oficina donde _____ un plato nuevo. (almorzar, probar)

6. Después de almorzar, _____ al trabajo donde _____ hasta las cuatro. (volver, quedarse)

6-19 Diario. Write a paragraph describing the last time you stayed in a hotel with someone. If you do not recall your last stay at a hotel with another person, imagine one.

In your paragraph, say...

- where you stayed.
- what time you went to bed, who woke up first, and how late the other person(s) slept.
- whether you got dressed immediately and left the hotel or stayed in the room a while.
- where you ate breakfast, lunch, and dinner and what you did all day.
- how much the room cost and how you paid.
- whether you liked the hotel.

_____

_____

_____

_____

_____

_____

¡A escuchar!

6-20 Una habitación de hotel. Listen to the following conversation in which a tourist is looking for a hotel room. Then complete these sentences according to what you hear in the dialogue.

1. Hay dos habitaciones _____ en el hotel.

2. Hay una habitación de _____ en el _____ piso y

   otra de no _____ en el _____ piso.

3. La habitación doble cuesta _____ pesos la noche y la habitación

   _____ cuesta _____ pesos la noche.

4. La turista prefiere la habitación más _____ porque prefiere una habitación de

   _____ .

6-21 ¿Por qué? A tourist who is traveling with his brother explains to a friend why his brother did things differently today. Give his answer to each question by putting the verb of the logical response from each pair in the preterite. Then listen and repeat as you hear the correct answer and write the verb form in the blank.

MODELO	You see:	_____ (dormir) hasta tarde _____ (vestirse) para salir
	You hear:	¿Por qué no desayunó contigo tu hermano?
	You say:	**No desayunó conmigo porque durmió hasta tarde.**
	You hear:	No desayunó conmigo porque durmió hasta tarde.
	You repeat:	**No desayunó conmigo porque durmió hasta tarde.**
	You write:	____**durmió**____ (dormir) hasta tarde _____ (vestirse) para salir

1. _____ (despertarse) tarde   _____ (viajar) conmigo

2. _____ (quedarse) en el hotel   _____ (acostarse) muy tarde anoche

3. _____ (preferir) dormir   _____ (divertirse) toda la noche

4. _____ (almorzar) en el hotel   _____ (salir) a un restaurante

5. _____ (vestirse) en el baño   _____ (pedir) algo que no le gustó

6. _____ (comer) muy poco   _____ (probar) un plato de la región

7. _____ (vestirse) en el baño   _____ (preferir) ir de compras

8. _____ (no cambiar) dinero   _____ (probarse) mucha ropa bonita

9. _____ (pedir) direcciones   _____ (no encontrar) un banco

10. _____ (perder) todas sus   _____ (preferir) las sandalias
    tarjetas de crédito   de cuero

Tema 4 ¿Qué tal la habitación?

6-22 En el hotel. Complete the following description of a guest's stay at a hotel. If there is a verb in parentheses, put it in the preterite. Otherwise fill in the blank with the logical word from the list.

camarera	sábanas	toallas	despertador	champú	papel higiénico	calefacción

(Yo) (1) _____ (despertarse) esta mañana a las seis y media cuando

(2) _____ (oír) mi (3) _____ y (yo)

(4) _____ (levantarse) inmediatamente. (Yo) (5) _____

(poner) la (6) _____ para no tener frío y (yo)

(7) _____ (ir) al baño para ducharme, pero no encontré

(8) _____ limpias. Llamé a la recepción y (9) _____

(pedir) más toallas y (10) _____ para lavarme el pelo. (Yo)

(11) _____ (sentarse) enfrente del televisor y (yo)

(12) _____ (ver) las noticias por unos minutos. Después de un rato la

(13) _____ me (14) _____ (traer) las toallas y el

champú. Luego, me duché, (15) _____ (vestirse) y salí a ver la ciudad. Estuve

fuera (*out*) del hotel varias horas y durante ese tiempo la camarera (16) _____

(volver) e (17) _____ (hacer) la cama y (18) _____

(poner) (19) _____ limpias. No entiendo por qué, pero también (ella)

(20) _____ (dejar) más de diez rollos de (21) _____

en el baño.

6-23 ¿Qué tiempo hizo? A tourist traveling across South America is saying what the weather was like in different places he and his friends visited. Complete each sentence with the preterite form of the indicated verb and the logical weather expression in parentheses.

MODELO   En Venezuela **estuvimos** (estar, nosotros) en la playa todo el tiempo porque **hizo calor** (llover, hacer calor) durante todo el viaje.

1. En Ecuador todos _____ (ponerse, nosotros) camiseta y sandalias porque

   _____ (hacer sol, nevar) todos los días. No _____
   (estar nublado, estar despejado) ni un solo día.

2. En Buenos Aires _____ (tener, nosotros) que comprar paraguas porque nadie

_____ (traer) uno y _____ (llover, hacer viento)

todo el tiempo.

3. En Chile _____ (poder, nosotros) esquiar porque

_____ (llover, nevar) mucho justo antes de nuestra llegada.

6-24 Un viaje de negocios (*business*). First read the following paragraph about a business trip. Then rewrite it, saying the same thing by substituting the verb from the list below it that conveys the same idea as each word in italics. The first one has been done as an example.

La semana pasada, Ramón Morales *viajó* a Asunción, Paraguay, por negocios. Su avión *despegó* a las ocho y cuarto de la mañana y *aterrizó en* Asunción a las cuatro de la tarde. Al llegar, un encargado (*staff member*) del hotel donde *se quedó* durante el viaje lo recogió en el aeropuerto. El primer día en Asunción, Ramón *asistió* a una conferencia sobre los últimos métodos de marketing internacional hasta las cuatro de la tarde, y luego *durmió una siesta* por dos horas antes de salir a cenar. Esa noche *se encontró en un restaurante* con otros hombres de negocios de la conferencia y todos *hablaron de* cosas muy interesantes relacionadas con su trabajo. Esa noche *regresó* muy cansado a su hotel y *se fue a dormir* inmediatamente. Ramón *tuvo* la misma rutina los cinco días que *se quedó* en Asunción. El sexto día *salió* temprano del hotel para ir al aeropuerto. Desafortunadamente, Ramón no *tuvo tiempo para* ver muchos sitios turísticos antes de volver a casa.

volver	alojarse	ir	cenar	hacer un viaje	salir	llegar a
estar	acostarse	descansar	repetir	irse	poder	decir

La semana pasada Ramón Morales _____**hizo un viaje**_____ a Asunción, Paraguay, por negocios. Su

avión (1) _____ a las ocho y cuarto de la mañana y

(2) _____ Asunción a las cuatro de la tarde. Al llegar, un encargado (*staff*

member) del hotel donde (3) _____ durante el viaje lo recogió en el aeropuerto. El

primer día en Asunción, Ramón (4) _____ a una conferencia sobre los últimos

métodos de marketing internacional hasta las cuatro de la tarde, y luego (5) _____

por dos horas antes de salir a cenar. Esa noche (6) _____ con otros hombres de

negocios de la conferencia y todos (7) _____ cosas muy interesantes relacionadas

con su trabajo. Esa noche (8) _____ muy cansado a su hotel y

(9) _____ inmediatamente. Ramón (10) _____ la

misma rutina los cinco días que (11) _____ en Asunción. El sexto día

(12) _____ temprano del hotel para ir al aeropuerto. Desafortunadamente,

Ramón no (13) _____ ver muchos sitios turísticos antes de volver a casa.

6-25 ¿Y tú? Imagine that a friend is asking you the following questions about your last vacation trip. Complete each question with the **tú** form of the verb, except in question 5. Then answer each question with a complete sentence in Spanish.

1. ¿Con quién _____ (hacer) el viaje?

   _____

2. ¿Adónde _____ (ir)?

   _____

3. ¿Cuánto tiempo _____ (estar) de vacaciones?

   _____

4. ¿_____ (tener) que tomar un avión o _____ (poder) viajar en coche?

   _____

5. ¿Qué tiempo _____ (hacer) durante el viaje?

   _____

6. ¿Qué ropa _____ (ponerse) generalmente durante el viaje?

   _____

7. ¿_____ (traer) a casa muchos recuerdos del viaje?

   _____

6-26 Diario. Write a paragraph in which you describe a trip you took for school, business, or for some other purpose besides leisure. Where did you go, with whom did you travel, and how did you get there? Were you able to see some historic sites and have some fun, or were you busy all of the time?

_____

_____

_____

_____

_____

_____

_____

¡A escuchar!

6-27 ¿No funciona o no hay? Listen as a hotel guest calls the front desk for service. Play the role of the receptionist and verify that something is missing or doesn't work in the room. Then listen and repeat as you hear the correct answer and mark **no hay** or **no funciona** on your paper.

MODELO   You hear: Estamos en la habitación 512 y no tenemos toallas limpias.
You say: **¿No hay toallas limpias en la habitación 512?**
You hear: ¿No hay toallas limpias en la habitación 512?
You repeat: **¿No hay toallas limpias en la habitación 512?**
You indicate: __X__ no hay _____ no funciona

1. _____ no hay   _____ no funciona   5. _____ no hay   _____ no funciona

2. _____ no hay   _____ no funciona   6. _____ no hay   _____ no funciona

3. _____ no hay   _____ no funciona   7. _____ no hay   _____ no funciona

4. _____ no hay   _____ no funciona   8. _____ no hay   _____ no funciona

6-28 Con los vecinos. Listen to a woman talk about her Saturday evening with her neighbors. Then stop the recording and write sentences saying who did the following things: **ella, sus vecinos,** or **nadie**.

MODELO   venir a su casa a cenar: **Sus vecinos vinieron a su casa a cenar.**

1. hacer mucha comida: _____.

2. traer un pastel: _____.

3. poner un CD: _____.

4. hacer mucho: _____.

5. estar en la casa hasta las nueve: _____.

6. tener que ir al aeropuerto: _____.

7. ponerse el pijama: _____.

6-29 Preguntas. Answer the following questions another student might ask you about last weekend with complete sentences in Spanish.

1. _____

2. _____

3. _____

4. _____

5. _____

Tema 5 ¿Conoce usted bien la ciudad?

6-30 Unos mandados. In which of the places from the list did a tourist do each of the following things? Write sentences in the **él/ella** form of the preterite.

el hotel   un teléfono público   la oficina de correos
el museo   la farmacia   el restaurante del hotel
la peluquería   el quiosco de periódicos   la gasolinera
la agencia de viajes   el banco   el teatro

MODELO   buscar una revista
               Buscó una revista en el quiosco de periódicos.

1. hacer una llamada internacional: _____

_____

2. dormir hasta tarde: _____

3. cortarse el pelo: _____

4. mandar unas tarjetas postales: _____

_____

5. probar un plato típico de la región: _____

_____

6. cambiar unos cheques de viaje: _____

_____

7. pedir medicamentos para las alergias: _____

8. poder encontrar información sobre las excursiones en la región: _____

_____

9. visitar una exposición: _____

10. ver una obra: _____

11. comprar gasolina: _____

6-31 En la recepción. Complete the following conversation between a hotel receptionist and a guest with the correct forms of **saber** or **conocer**.

El huésped: Perdón, señor. (Yo) no (1) _____ muy bien la ciudad y

necesito comprar unos medicamentos. ¿(2) _____ Ud.
dónde hay una farmacia cerca de aquí?

El recepcionista: ¿(3) _____ Ud. la plaza Hidalgo?

El huésped: No, (yo) no (4) _____ dónde está. Acabo de llegar en taxi y

(yo) no (5) _____ el barrio.

El recepcionista: Si va a la izquierda al salir del hotel, está a cuatro cuadras de aquí. En esa plaza hay una

farmacia, pero (yo) no (6) _____ si está abierta a esta hora
o no.

6-32 En mi familia. Say who in your family knows how to do each of the pictured activities.

MODELO **Yo sé esquiar. / Mi padre sabe esquiar. / Mi padre y yo sabemos esquiar. /
Todos sabemos esquiar. / Nadie sabe esquiar.**

Modelo   1.   2.

3.   4.   5.

1. _____

2. _____

3. _____

4. _____

5. _____

Nombre: _____ Fecha: _____

6-33 ¿Saber o conocer? You are planning a trip to Europe with a friend who asks you the following questions. Complete each one with the **tú** form of **saber** or **conocer**. Then answer each question about yourself.

1. ¿Qué lenguas _____ hablar?

   _____

2. ¿_____ a alguien de España o de Francia?

   _____

3. ¿_____ en qué países se usa el euro?

   _____

4. ¿_____ algunos sitios históricos en España?

   _____

5. ¿_____ qué tiempo hace ahora en Madrid?

   _____

6-34 Diario. Write a paragraph explaining where someone can run various errands around your university. Mention as many of the places presented on page 180 of the textbook as you can and explain where they are located. If you are not familiar with one of those places near the university, say so using **No conozco ningún/ninguna...** or **No sé dónde hay... en el barrio**.

_____
_____
_____
_____
_____
_____
_____
_____
_____
_____

¡A escuchar!

6-35 Dificultades. Some tourists had trouble doing what they wanted because they could not find the right places. Complete what they say with the preterite form of **poder** and the logical place from each pair shown. Then listen and repeat as you hear the correct answer and indicate the place named.

MODELO   You see: _____ una farmacia   _____ una oficina de correos

You hear: Fuimos a mandar unas cartas.

You say: **Fuimos a mandar unas cartas pero no pudimos encontrar una oficina de correos.**

You hear: Fuimos a mandar unas cartas pero no pudimos encontrar una oficina de correos.

You repeat: **Fuimos a mandar unas cartas pero no pudimos encontrar una oficina de correos.**

You indicate: _____ una farmacia   **X** una oficina de correos

1. _____ una agencia de viajes   _____ una peluquería

2. _____ una oficina de correos   _____ una librería

3. _____ una farmacia abierta   _____ un café abierto

4. _____ un banco abierto   _____ un restaurante abierto

5. _____ un teléfono público   _____ un hotel

6-36 ¿Me podría decir...? Listen to a conversation in which a tourist is asking a hotel receptionist for directions. Then complete the following statements according to what you hear in the dialogue.

1. El turista busca una _____ para comprar una _____.

2. Para llegar al lugar que busca, debe ir a la _____ al _____

   del hotel. Necesita _____ tres _____.

3. El turista también quiere comprar un _____.

4. Si no lo tienen en el primer lugar, el turista puede comprarlo en un _____

   a una _____ del hotel a la _____.

6-37 En el taxi. Listen to a conversation between a tourist and a taxi driver. Then complete the following sentences according to what you hear.

1. El taxista conoce _____.

2. El taxista no conoce _____.

3. El taxista sabe dónde _____.

4. El taxista no sabe cuánto _____.

¡Trato hecho!

6-38 En la red. On the Internet, search for vacation packages in two different Hispanic countries by searching for *paquetes de vacaciones en [name of country]* or *paquetes de viaje en [name of country]*. List the addresses of the interesting sites that you find and give the information indicated below.

www._____

www._____

Paquete de vacaciones 1

Lugar: _____

Duración: _____

Precio: _____

Alojamiento: _____

Actividades: _____

_____

_____

_____

Paquete de vacaciones 2

Lugar: _____

Duración: _____

Precio: _____

Alojamiento: _____

Actividades: _____

_____

_____

_____

6-39 Composición. Imagine that you spent your vacation in one of the places you described in the preceding section and now you are writing an e-mail to a friend talking about what you did while on vacation. Include the following information:

- where you went and with whom
- when you left and when you returned
- a description of your flight when you went and returned
- where you stayed and whether you liked it
- four or five things that you did while there
- what you bought and how much you spent in total (**en total**)

_____

_____

_____

_____

_____

_____

_____

_____

_____

_____

_____

_____

_____

_____

_____

_____

7   En la ciudad

Tema 1 ¿Cómo eras de niño/a?

7-1 Profesiones. Name the profession shown in each illustration. Be sure to use the correct form of *a(n)* (**un, una**) or *some* (**unos, unas**).

1.

2.

3.

4.

5.

6.

7.

8.

9.

10.

1. _____

2. _____

3. _____

4. _____

5. _____

6. _____

7. _____

8. _____

9. _____

10. _____

7-2 ¿A qué se dedican? Form sentences in Spanish by linking each profession to the appropriate job description. Conjugate the verb **dedicarse a** as necessary.

una actriz		enseñar a los niños
los maestros		hacer música
un deportista		ayudar a los enfermos
los obreros de la construcción	dedicarse a	hacer teatro
un enfermero		construir casas
un músico		practicar deportes

1. _____

2. _____

3. _____

4. _____

5. _____

6. _____

7-3 Las montañas. A friend is recounting what life was like when he was a child. Complete his description with the correct imperfect form of an appropriate verb from the list. You may use the same verb twice.

escuchar	gustar	hablar	hacer	jugar	leer
pasar	pasear	tener	tocar	ver	vivir

Cuando yo (1) _____ cinco años, nuestra familia

(2) _____ con mis abuelos en las montañas. Yo no

(3) _____ muchos amigos allí, pero (4) _____ mucho

con mi hermano mayor sobre cosas nuestras. Mi hermano mayor (5) _____ la

guitarra, y a veces por la noche, yo (6) _____ la radio. Mi hermano y yo no

(7) _____ la televisión, porque en esos días nos

(8) _____ explorar por las montañas. Mi madre (9) _____

muchos libros mientras mi padre y mi abuelo (10) _____ al ajedrez. Mis padres

(11) _____ muchas cosas juntos. A veces ellos

(12) _____ por la tarde y (13) _____ de su día. Mi

familia (14) _____ más tiempo junta antes.

7-4 ¡Qué cambio! Soledad has changed her habits a lot since she was a child. Read what her habits are now and write the opposite for her childhood, using the imperfect tense. Also explain why, using one of the reasons from the list.

vivir en un vecindario con muchas familias   no tener televisor en casa
ser muy religiosa   no tener mucha tarea para la escuela
ser muy curiosa sobre todos   siempre querer jugar con alguien

MODELO   Ahora Soledad ve mucho la televisión.
               Cuando era niña, Soledad no veía mucho la televisión porque no tenía televisor en casa.

1. A Soledad le gusta pasar tiempo sola.

   _____

2. Soledad nunca va a misa (*mass*) los domingos.

   _____

3. Soledad es muy tímida con las personas que no conoce.

   _____

4. Soledad no tiene mucho tiempo libre para estar con sus amigos.

   _____

5. No hay muchos niños en el vecindario de Soledad.

   _____

7-5 Diario. Write two paragraphs describing how you were as a child. Did you use to behave well? What sports did you like/play? What did you dream of doing? How is your life now different from your life as a child?

_____

_____

_____

_____

_____

_____

_____

_____

¡A escuchar!

7-6 La familia de Jorge. Listen to Jorge describe different family members when he was a child. Repeat each sentence you hear and complete the corresponding statement with the logical profession of the person described.

MODELO   You see: Mi padre era _____.

                  You hear: Mi padre trabajaba con los médicos en un hospital.

                  You repeat: **Mi padre trabajaba con los médicos en un hospital.**

                  You write: Mi padre era **enfermero.**

1. Mi abuelo era _____.

2. Mi madre era _____.

3. Mi hermano quería ser _____.

4. Mis hermanas soñaban con ser _____.

5. Mi tío era _____.

6. Mi abuela era _____.

7-7 De niño y ahora. Listen to the following statements that Fernando says about his life now and his life as a child. Mark **ahora** for the statements referring to the present and **de niño** for the statements referring to his childhood.

1. ___ ahora	___ de niño	4. ___ ahora	___ de niño	7. ___ ahora	___ de niño
2. ___ ahora	___ de niño	5. ___ ahora	___ de niño	8. ___ ahora	___ de niño
3. ___ ahora	___ de niño	6. ___ ahora	___ de niño	9. ___ ahora	___ de niño

Now play the statements again and change them to describe your childhood if they are in the imperfect, and to describe you now if they are in the present tense. If they already describe you, write them as you hear them.

1. _____

2. _____

3. _____

4. _____

5. _____

6. _____

7. _____

8. _____

9. _____

Tema 2 Los grandes acontecimientos de la vida

7-8 Acontecimientos. Complete each sentence below with the word from the list for the event described.

cumpleaños	jubilación	concurso	boda	funeral
nacimiento	graduación	licencia de manejar		

1. Los abuelos se sienten muy orgullosos con el _____ de su nieto.

2. Todos los novios están muy emocionados el día de su _____.

3. Los niños se divierten en su fiesta de _____.

4. Las familias están muy tristes en el _____ de algún ser querido (*loved one*).

5. Estoy muy contento de tener mi _____. Me gusta manejar.

6. Mi padre tiene más tiempo libre después de su _____.

7. Los estudiantes se sienten muy orgullosos el día de su _____ de la escuela.

8. La deportista está nerviosa por el _____ de patinaje.

7-9 ¿Qué pasó? Make logical sentences by linking the statements in the left column with the appropriate ending from the right column.

1. _____ Cuando tenía siete años

2. _____ Mis padres se conocieron

3. _____ Cuando se graduaron de la universidad

4. _____ Cuando éramos niños

5. _____ Saqué mi licencia de manejar

6. _____ Conocí a mi mejor amigo

a. cuando estaba en el colegio.

b. gané mi primer concurso de belleza.

c. vivíamos en San Francisco.

d. cuando cumplí dieciséis años.

e. cuando eran muy jóvenes.

f. estaban muy nerviosos.

Now complete the following sentences so that they describe you.

1. Cuando tenía siete años, _____.

2. Mis padres se conocieron _____.

3. Cuando me gradué de la escuela secundaria, _____.

4. Cuando éramos niños, _____.

5. Saqué mi licencia de manejar _____.

6. Conocí a mi mejor amigo _____.

7-10 El día de su graduación. Esperanza talks about her brother Eduardo's graduation. Complete her statements by writing the logical verb in each blank, using the imperfect for what was already in progress, and the preterite for what happened.

MODELO   Yo **tenía** doce años cuando mi hermano Eduardo **se graduó** de la universidad. (graduarse, tener)

1. Toda mi familia _____ a su graduación y mis padres

   _____ muy orgullosos. (ir, estar)

2. El día de la graduación _____ e _____ muy mal

   tiempo cuando (nosotros) _____. (llover, llegar, hacer)

3. Mi hermano _____ la toga mientras (nosotros) _____
   el comienzo de la ceremonia. (ponerse, esperar)

4. Mis padres _____ muchas fotos de mi hermano porque

   _____ muy guapo en la toga. (sacar, estar)

5. Mi hermano nos _____ cuando _____ con los otros

   estudiantes porque (nosotros) _____ cerca de la entrada. (estar, ver, entrar).

6. Mis padres y yo _____ a la novia de mi hermano mientras

   _____ la fiesta de Eduardo. (celebrar, conocer)

7. Mi hermano y ella _____ cuando mis padres y yo los

   _____. (abrazarse, ver)

7-11 ¡Qué triste! Andrés is telling Gema about his sister's wedding. Complete the conversation with the appropriate verb from the list below in the preterite or imperfect, as necessary.

| perder | celebrarse | beber | empezar | despertarse | sentirse | nevar | esperar | manejar |

— ¡Andrés! ¿Qué tal la boda de tu hermana?

— Ay, Gema, fue un desastre. El sábado cuando nosotros (1) _____,

(2) _____. Por eso, casi nadie vino a la boda.

— ¡Qué pena!

— Sí, y después mientras los invitados (3) _____ al novio en la iglesia, mi

hermano pequeño (4) _____ los anillos, y mi padre estaba muy enojado con él.

— Oh, pobre Arturo.

— Eso no es todo. Cuando (5) _____ la ceremonia, mi hermana

(6) _____ mal y tuvo que salir de la iglesia.

— Mis padres no sabían qué hacer y mi madre empezó a llorar.

— ¿Y tu hermana?

— Mientras los invitados (7) _____ el champán, mis padres y yo

(8) _____ al hospital para llevar a mi hermana a ver a un médico.

— ¿Y la boda no (9) _____?

— No, pero la recepción sí. ¡Sin los novios!

7-12 Diario. Write a paragraph talking about an important event in your life and in the life of your loved ones. How old were you when these events occurred? What were the circumstances? How did you feel about what occurred?

_____

_____

_____

_____

_____

_____

¡A escuchar!

7-13 ¿Qué acontecimiento? Listen and repeat the following statements and indicate the event that is described with an **X.**

MODELO: You see: _____ la boda   _____ el cumpleaños
You hear: Mis amigos vinieron a mi fiesta cuando cumplí siete años.
You repeat: **Mis amigos vinieron a mi fiesta cuando cumplí siete años.**
You indicate: _____ la boda   __X__ el cumpleaños

1. _____ la boda   _____ el funeral

2. _____ la graduación   _____ la jubilación

3. _____ el nacimiento   _____ el funeral

4. _____ el campeonato   _____ la licencia de manejar

5. _____ la boda   _____ la jubilación

6. _____ la quinceañera   _____ el funeral

7. _____ el nacimiento   _____ la licencia de manejar

8. _____ el cumpleaños   _____ el nacimiento

7-14 ¡Qué buenos recuerdos! Listen to the following conversation in which a person is talking about his best memories when he was younger. Then complete the following sentences according to what you hear in the dialogue.

1. Cuando tenía nueve años, mi equipo _____ el campeonato de fútbol.

2. Cuando _____ el gol, estaba muy orgulloso.

3. Cuando estaba en la escuela secundaria, _____ a mi mejor amigo.

4. Cuando _____ en la clase de español, mi profesora nos llevó de viaje a España.

5. Cuando empezamos en la universidad, mi amigo _____ a Rhode Island para estudiar allí.

6. Cuando mi hermana _____, mi amigo asistió a la boda.

Tema 3 Mis cuentos preferidos

7-15 Mi cuento favorito. Complete the following sentences with the logical verbs from the list in the preterite or the imperfect.

ahogar	encontrar	contar	oír	arrepentirse	gustar	volver	ser

1. Cuando era niña me _____ leer cuentos.

2. Mi abuela siempre me _____ cuentos antes de dormir.

3. Mi cuento favorito _____ la historia de La Llorona.

4. La Llorona _____ a sus hijos en el río.

5. Después la Llorona _____ de matar a sus hijos.

6. Unos niños del pueblo _____ a la Llorona muerta en la orilla del río.

7. El fantasma de la Llorona _____ para buscar a sus hijos.

8. Después de ese día los campesinos _____ cada noche un llanto triste del río.

7-16 La Malinche. Complete the beginning of the true story of **la Malinche** by selecting the correct verb form from those given in parentheses.

La Malinche (1) (nació / nacía) en la región de Coatzalcoacos, en el sur de México. Su padre (2) (fue / era) un cacique azteca y de niña (3) (se llamó / se llamaba) Malintzin. Su padre (4) (murió / moría) cuando (5) (fue / era) muy joven y su madre (6) (volvió / volvía) a casarse y (7) (tuvo / tenía) un hijo con su segundo esposo. Para evitar cuestiones de sucesión, la madre de Malintzin y su padrastro la (8) (vendieron / vendían) a unos mercaderes de esclavos (*slave merchants*). Sus padres (9) (dijeron / decían) que (10) (estuvo / estaba) muerta y (11) (celebraron / celebraban) su entierro falso en público con mucha tristeza.

    Los mercaderes de esclavos (12) (vendieron / vendían) a Malintzin a un cacique maya de Tabasco, donde (13) (vivió / vivía) hasta la edad de 20 años. Cuando Hernán Cortés (14) (llegó / llegaba) a la región de Tabasco en 1519, los mayas de la región se la (15) (ofrecieron / ofrecían) con 20 esclavas como ofrenda de paz (*peace offering*) y los españoles le (16) (pusieron / ponían) el nombre de Marina. Cuando Cortés (17) (supo / sabía) que Marina (18) (supo / sabía) hablar maya y nahuatl, la lengua de los aztecas, y además (19) (conoció / conocía) sus culturas, (20) (entendió / entendía) que (21) (fue / era) muy útil. Más tarde Cortés (22) (dijo / decía) "Marina (23) (fue / era) un gran principio para nuestra conquista".

7-17 Cortés y Marina. Now complete the story of **la Malinche** by writing the verbs in parentheses in the appropriate form of the preterite or the imperfect.

Marina (1) _____ (aprender) el español muy pronto y Cortés la (2) _____

(hacer) su traductora. Como (3) _____ (sentir) odio (*hatred*) por su pueblo de origen, no

sólo (4) _____ (traducir), sino que les (5) _____ (ofrecer) información sobre la sociedad y la cultura de los aztecas para poder conquistarlos. Cortés y sus soldados

(6) _____ (vencer *to defeat*) a los aztecas en 1521 y dos años después la Malinche, como la

(7) _____ (llamar) los indígenas, (8) _____ (tener) un hijo de Cortés,

Martín Cortés. Ese mismo año, los españoles (9) _____ (convocar *to summon*) a todos los

caciques para convertirlos al cristianismo y (10) _____ (venir) el medio hermano y la

madrastra de la Malinche. Su padrastro ya (11) _____ (estar) muerto. Su madre y su medio

hermano (12) _____ (creer) que los españoles los (13) _____ (ir) a

matar, pero cuando la Malinche (14) _____ (ver) que (15) _____ (llorar)

los (16) _____ (consolar) y (17) _____ (abrazar) a su madre.

En 1524, Cortés (18) _____ (salir) con la Malinche a conquistar Honduras. La

expedición (19) _____ (ser) un desastre. Muchos hombres (20) _____

(morir) y Cortés (21) _____ (perder) su poder (*power*). (22) _____

(entregar *to hand over*) a la Malinche a otro soldado español y no se supo más de su vida.

7-18 El día de Analissa. Read the description of Analissa's day below and change the sentences from the present to the imperfect or preterite as appropriate to the context.

Por la mañana
1. Cuando suena el despertador, Analissa tiene mucho sueño y duerme un poco más.
2. No tiene tiempo para desayunar y compra un café en la calle.
3. Hace buen tiempo y decide caminar a la oficina.
4. Cuando llega a la oficina, su jefe está esperándola.

Por la tarde
5. Sale a almorzar con Paquita pero la comida en el restaurante es muy mala.
6. Hay mucho que hacer en la oficina y trabaja toda la tarde sin descanso.
7. No tiene mucha energía y se siente muy cansada.
8. No puede terminar el trabajo y se lo lleva a casa.

Por la noche
9. Asiste a una fiesta de jubilación de un compañero.
10. Después de la fiesta, vuelve a casa. Está muy cansada.
11. Quiere ver una película, pero no hay nada bueno en la televisión.
12. Se acuesta temprano y se duerme pronto.

1. _____

2. _____

3. _____

4. _____

5. _____

6. _____

7. _____

8. _____

9. _____

10. _____

11. _____

12. _____

7-19 Diario. Write a paragraph about your favorite tale when you were a child. Use the imperfect to describe the characters, the background, and the circumstances of the story, and the preterite to narrate the sequence of events.

_____

_____

_____

_____

_____

_____

_____

_____

_____

_____

_____

_____

_____

_____

¡A escuchar!

7-20 Mi boda. Listen to Ana tell how she met her husband and the details about their wedding. Then answer the following questions according to what you hear.

1. ¿Dónde vivía Ana en el año 2000? ¿Qué hacía allí?

   _____

2. Durante sus años de universidad, ¿qué hacía Ana durante la semana? ¿Qué hacía los fines de semana?

   _____

3. Una noche el chef del restaurante se enfermó. ¿Qué solución encontró Laura, la amiga de Ana?

   _____

4. ¿A quién conoció Ana aquella noche?

   _____

5. ¿Cuánto tiempo fueron novios Ana y Rubén?

   _____

6. ¿Cuándo y dónde se casaron?

   _____

7. ¿Cómo fue la boda?

   _____

7-21 ¿Qué heroína? Indicate which of the following characters from stories for children is being described in each statement that you hear.

1. _____ La Cenicienta _____ La Guanina _____ Pocahontas _____ La Llorona

2. _____ La Cenicienta _____ La Guanina _____ Pocahontas _____ La Llorona

3. _____ La Cenicienta _____ La Guanina _____ Pocahontas _____ La Llorona

4. _____ La Cenicienta _____ La Guanina _____ Pocahontas _____ La Llorona

Tema 4 ¿Cómo era el vecindario?

7-22 El centro de la ciudad. Look at the illustration below and name the different people and places as appropriate. Be sure to use the correct form of *a(n)* (**un, una**) or *some* (**unos, unas**).

1. _____   9. _____

2. _____   10. _____

3. _____   11. _____

4. _____   12. _____

5. _____   13. _____

6. _____   14. _____

7. _____   15. _____

8. _____   16. _____

7-23 ¿Qué se hace? Write what people generally do in each situation using the **se impersonal**.

MODELO   En el semáforo rojo **se espera un poco.**

conocer a todos los vecinos   arreglar autos   respirar más aire contaminado   manejar rápido
guardar (*to keep*) los carros   esperar un poco   esperar el autobús

1. En la parada de autobús, _____.

2. En el taller, _____.

3. En las autopistas, _____.

4. En el barrio, _____.

5. En la ciudad, _____.

6. En el estacionamiento, _____.

7-24 Antes y hoy. Explain which actions used to happen in the past using **antes** and the imperfect, and which happen nowadays using **hoy** and the present tense. Use the **se impersonal** in your sentences, as in the **modelo**.

MODELO   comer en restaurantes con frecuencia / cocinar en casa
          Antes se cocinaba más en casa y hoy se come en restaurantes con frecuencia.

1. jugar mucho en la calle / mirar demasiado la televisión

_____

2. vivir más tranquilo en la ciudad / necesitar tener cuidado con el tráfico

_____

3. manejar más / poder andar mucho a pie

_____

4. hacer autopistas grandes / ver más espacios verdes

_____

5. ver menos accidentes en las calles / encontrar choques de autos todos los días

_____

7-25 Hace cincuenta años. Imagine how life was fifty years ago and respond to the following questions using the **se impersonal** in your answers.

MODELO   ¿Hacían las personas edificios altos?
            No, no se hacían edificios altos.

1. ¿Respiraban las personas aire más fresco?

_____

2. ¿Pasaban los conductores muchas horas en el tráfico?

_____

3. ¿Preparaban las mujeres la comida en la casa?

_____

4. ¿Ponía la policía muchas multas?

_____

5. ¿Vivían las personas mejor?

_____

7-26 Diario. Write two paragraphs comparing what students used to do when you were in high school during the week and on the weekends, and what people usually do now at the university. Use the **se impersonal** in your descriptions.

_____

_____

_____

_____

_____

_____

_____

_____

_____

_____

¡A escuchar!

7-27 Buenos Aires. You will hear a series of statements about Buenos Aires. Indicate whether each statement is true or false by marking **cierto** or **falso**. Then rewrite each false statement to make it true. Read the *Escapadas* section on pages 222-223 of the textbook to help you with this exercise.

MODELO   You hear: En el barrio de La Boca se creó el tango.
                You mark: __X__ cierto _____ falso

1. _____ cierto _____ falso _____

2. _____ cierto _____ falso _____

3. _____ cierto _____ falso _____

4. _____ cierto _____ falso _____

5. _____ cierto _____ falso _____

6. _____ cierto _____ falso _____

7-28 ¿Qué es apropiado? Listen to the following questions and answer them negatively, using the **se impersonal** and the cue in your answer. Then listen to the correct answer.

MODELO   You see: escuchar la música muy baja
                You hear: ¿Escuchan las personas la música muy alta en los hospitales?
                You write: **No, en los hospitales se escucha la música muy baja**.
                You hear: No, en los hospitales se escucha la música muy baja.

1. manejar a alta velocidad

    _____

2. dejar los autos en un estacionamiento

    _____

3. andar a pie por la acera

    _____

4. esperar el autobús en la parada del autobús

    _____

5. dar multas a los conductores

    _____

6. respirar aire contaminado

    _____

Tema 5 ¿Vio usted lo que pasó?

7-29 ¿Qué hacer? Complete the following advice given in case you witness or are involved in a car accident. Use the vocabulary words from page 214 of the textbook.

En caso de accidente de carretera

- Usted debe llamar a la policía si ve una (1) _____ en la carretera.

- Si usted maneja por la carretera y ve dos coches que acaban de (2) _____,

  llame a la (3) _____.

- Usted no debe mover a las (4) _____; debe esperar a los

  (5) _____.

- Usted puede administrar los (6) _____ si sabe cómo hacerlo, mientras

  llega una (7) _____.

- Si sale humo de los coches, llame a los (8) _____. No debe sacar a los

  (9) _____ de los coches usted solo.

7-30 Un robo. Complete the following conversation between Elisa and Paco with the preterite or imperfect forms of the verbs in parentheses.

— Hola Elisa, soy Paco. ¿Estás bien? ¿Por qué no (1) _____ (venir) a clase hoy?

— Hola Paco, gracias por llamar. No fui a clase hoy porque ayer (2) _____ (ser) víctima de un robo (*robbery*).

— ¿En serio? ¿Cuándo (3) _____ (ocurrir) el robo?

— Ayer por la noche, cuando (4) _____ (volver) de mis clases. Andaba a mi casa

  cuando un criminal me (5) _____ (asaltar).

— Y ¿resultaste herida?

— No, pero (6) _____ (venir) una ambulancia para llevarme primero al hospital y después a casa.

— Y ¿(7) _____ (haber) testigos del robo?

— No, nadie (8) _____ (ver) lo que ocurrió. Llamé a la policía para poner una denuncia, pero todavía no se ha hecho (*hasn't been done*) ningún arresto.

Capítulo 7 • En la ciudad **149**

7-31 El informe del accidente. Complete the following accident report with the appropriate forms of the verbs in the preterite or the imperfect, according to the context.

La Srta. Silva (1) _____ (ir) hacia el norte en su vehículo en la Avenida Portillo y

(2) _____ (girar) a la izquierda en el semáforo de la Calle Ocho. El Sr. Mújica,

conductor del otro coche, (3) _____ (venir) a exceso de velocidad desde el oeste

en la Calle Ocho y no (4) _____ (poder) parar (*to stop*) en la luz roja. Como

resultado, los dos coches (5) _____ (chocar). Nadie

(6) _____ (resultar) herido. Sólo (7) _____ (haber

[hay]) daños (*damage*) en los dos vehículos, principalmente en el maletero (*trunk*) del coche de la Srta. Silva

y en la puerta izquierda del coche del Sr. Mújica. Ni la Srta. Silva ni el Sr. Mújica

(8) _____ (estar) asegurados (*insured*) con ninguna compañía. Pronto

(9) _____ (llegar) una grúa para llevarse los coches.

7-32 ¿Cómo ocurrió? A policewoman is asking you about the following accident that you witnessed. Complete the questions about the incident with a form of the verb in the preterite or imperfect. Then answer each question according to the illustrations.

1. ¿Qué _____ (hacer) la conductora del carro cuando

   _____ (chocar)?

_____

2. ¿Ella _____ (estar) sola en el carro o _____ (estar) con amigos?

_____

3. ¿Por qué no _____ (parar *to stop*) en el semáforo en rojo?

¿_____ (manejar) rápido?

_____

4. ¿_____ (resultar) alguien herido en el accidente?

_____

5. ¿_____ (haber) más gente (*people*) en la calle?

¿_____ (ver) el accidente?

_____

7-33 Diario. Did you ever witness a car accident? Did you ever witness a fire? Were you ever a victim of an assault? Write two paragraphs describing one of these situations that you might have witnessed or have been the victim of, using the vocabulary from **Tema 5** and the appropriate past tenses. You may also imagine such an incident, if you prefer.

_____

_____

_____

_____

_____

_____

_____

_____

_____

_____

_____

_____

¡A escuchar!

7-34 911, ¿en qué puedo ayudarle? Listen and complete the following phone conversation between a 911 operator and a person who just witnessed an accident.

— 911, ¿en qué puedo ayudarle?

— Sí, hola, llamo por una (1) _____. Un coche acaba de

   (2) _____ contra un letrero, y el conductor parece estar

   (3) _____.

— ¿Dónde (4) _____ el accidente?

— En la intersección de las calles Alberto Aguilera y Princesa, en la esquina

   (5) _____ al Corte Inglés.

— Muy bien, ahora mando una (6) _____.

— ¿Hubo otros (7) _____ en el lugar del accidente?

— Sí, varias personas que iban a (8) _____ la calle, y una motocicleta que

   esperaba en el (9) _____ rojo.

— ¿Alguna de estas personas (10) _____ herida?

— No, sólo el conductor del coche.

7-35 El incendio. Imagine that there was a fire in your apartment and one of your friends is asking you questions about the incident. Complete the answers you see with the appropriate verbs in the past tense.

MODELO You see: No, _____ en la universidad cuando _____ el incendio.
        You hear: ¿Estabas en casa cuando ocurrió el incendio?
        You write: No, **estaba** en la universidad cuando **ocurrió** el incendio.

1. No, no _____ el gas de la cocina cuando _____ de
   casa esta mañana.

2. No, no _____ mucho humo por las ventanas.

3. No, no _____ del incendio por la policía, me _____
   un vecino.

4. No, ningún vecino _____ herido.

5. No, no _____ el seguro (*insurance*) de mi apartamento este año.

6. No, no _____ salvar nada. Todo está perdido.

¡Trato hecho!

7-36 En la red. Search the web for important celebrations for Hispanics such as *la quinceañera* and *el cumpleaños*. You can extend your search entering *quinceañera* with *tradicional* (but not as a string) or *la piñata* with *origen* (but not as a string). Check the sites you find for the information requested below and answer the questions in English. Write down the addresses of the interesting and useful sites you discover and share them with your instructor and other students.

Addresses of useful and interesting sites:

www._____

www._____

www._____

1. What is **la quinceañera**? What was the traditional **quinceañera** like?

   _____

   _____

   _____

2. What does this traditional ceremony symbolize? Do young Hispanic women living in the United States still celebrate **la quinceañera**?

   _____

   _____

   _____

3. What is a **piñata**? What is the origin of **la piñata**? Name some celebrations in which **la piñata** is present.

   _____

   _____

   _____

4. Name a popular celebration among American teenagers and what traditions are involved.

   _____

   _____

   _____

7-37 Composición. Using what you have learned in this chapter, write a composition describing your favorite celebration when you were a child. What time of the year did the celebration take place? What did the celebration consist of? Who used to attend this celebration? What made this celebration so special for you? Then describe what happened on one memorable occasion when you were celebrating it.

_____

_____

_____

_____

_____

_____

_____

_____

_____

_____

_____

_____

_____

_____

_____

_____

_____

_____

8   En el restaurante

Tema 1 ¿Qué me recomienda?

8-1 En la mesa. Write the names of the indicated objects from the illustration with the appropriate indefinite article (**un, una**).

a. _____

b. _____

c. _____

d. _____

e. _____

f. _____

g. _____

h. _____   j. _____

i. _____   k. _____

8-2 ¿Para qué se usa? Which objects from the list in the preceding activity are used for the following purposes? Write the corresponding letters in the blanks. In some cases more than one may be used.

MODELO   _**g, i, j**_ para cortar el bistec

1. _____ para tomar agua   4. _____ para servir vino

2. _____ para tomar sopa (*soup*) 5. _____ para proteger la mesa

3. _____ para tomar café   6. _____ para limpiarse las manos o la boca (*mouth*)

8-3 Me das... How would you ask a friend to give you the pictured objects? Include the indirect object pronoun, as in the **modelo**.

MODELO   **¿Me das una taza de té, por favor?**

1.   2.   3.   4.

Capítulo 8 • En el restaurante   **155**

1. _____

2. _____

3. _____

4. _____

8-4 En el restaurante. Write the names of the pictured objects in the blanks with the definite article (**el, la**).

1. _____

2. _____

3. _____

4. _____

5. _____

6. _____

7. _____

8-5 ¿Qué hacían? The illustration in the preceding activity is the scene you found when you arrived at the restaurant. With whom were these people interacting? Write sentences using indirect object pronouns with the indicated verbs in the imperfect.

MODELO   el cocinero / explicar algo
              El cocinero le explicaba algo al dueño.

1. Arturo / proponer matrimonio: _____

2. Mónica / contestar que sí: _____

3. Javier / dar la cuenta: _____

4. Orlando, Fernanda y Juan / pedir la comida: _____

5. la mesera / describir el plato del día: _____

6. el mesero / ofrecer postres: _____

7. Carlos e Isabel / dejar una propina: _____

8-6 ¡Qué buen servicio! Complete the following sentences by writing the logical verb in each blank, using the preterite and the appropriate indirect object pronoun.

MODELO   El mesero **nos dio** el menú y nosotros **le pedimos** la comida. (pedir, dar)

1. Yo ____ _____ qué prefería él y ____ _____ la paella. (preguntar, recomendar)

2. El mesero ____ _____ si podía retirar mi plato sucio y ____

   _____ que sí. (preguntar, contestar)

3. Mi amigo ____ _____ un trozo de pastel al mesero, pero yo ____

   _____ que no quería postre. (decir, pedir)

4. El mesero ____ _____ la cuenta a mí, pero yo ____

   _____ que mi amigo iba a pagar. (decir, dar)

5. El mesero ____ _____ muy buen servicio, entonces nosotros ____

   _____ una buena propina. (dejar, dar)

8-7 Diario. Using the preterite and the imperfect, describe the last time that you ate at a restaurant where a server waited on you. Include the following information:

- where you ate and whether you ate breakfast, lunch, or dinner
- whether there were many people when you arrived, what they were doing, and whether you had to wait long (**mucho tiempo**)
- what the service was like, whether the server gave you menus, whether you asked him/her questions, and whether he/she recommended anything in particular
- what you ordered and whether the server brought it to you quickly
- whether the waiter removed your plates when you finished and recommended desserts to you
- whether you paid the server or you paid the check at the register
- whether you left the waiter a tip

_____

_____

_____

_____

_____

_____

_____

¡A escuchar!

8-8 En el restaurante. Listen to a series of questions you might hear at a Mexican restaurant. Answer each question with the logical response from the list. Then, as you hear the correct answer, repeat it and write the number of the question in the blank next to it.

MODELO You hear: ¿Están listos o necesitan más tiempo?
You say: **No, necesitamos ver el menú un poco más.**
You hear: No, necesitamos ver el menú un poco más.
You repeat: **No, necesitamos ver el menú un poco más.**
You indicate: *The number of the question next to it.*

_____ a. Las de harina para mí, pero mi amigo prefiere las de maíz.

_____ b. Sí, gracias, ya terminamos.

_____ c. Tenemos flan, pastel de queso y helado de vainilla, fresa o chocolate.

_____ d. Quiero las enchiladas suizas y mi amigo quiere los tacos al carbón.

Modelo e. No, necesitamos ver el menú un poco más.

_____ f. Vienen con frijoles y arroz.

_____ g. Sólo la cuenta, por favor.

_____ h. Sí, cómo no, con identificación.

_____ i. Sí, incluye el servicio.

_____ j. Un agua mineral para mí y un vino tinto para mi amigo.

Now play the questions again and indicate whether the server or the customer is asking each one.

1. ____ el mesero ____ el cliente 4. ____ el mesero ____ el cliente 7. ____ el mesero ____ el cliente

2. ____ el mesero ____ el cliente 5. ____ el mesero ____ el cliente 8. ____ el mesero ____ el cliente

3. ____ el mesero ____ el cliente 6. ____ el mesero ____ el cliente 9. ____ el mesero ____ el cliente

8-9 ¿Y tú? Answer each question a friend might ask with a complete sentence in Spanish.

1. _____

2. _____

3. _____

4. _____

5. _____

Tema 2 ¿Qué desea usted?

8-10 ¿Qué se le pone? Would a person normally say he/she puts salt, sugar, and/or butter on or in the following foods or drinks? Note in the **modelo** how the indirect object is used with **poner** to express this, and write a similar sentence for each item shown.

MODELO 1 **Le pongo azúcar al té.**

MODELO 2 **Les pongo sal y mantequilla a las papas al horno.**

1.   2.   3.   4.   5.   6.

1. _____

2. _____

3. _____

4. _____

5. _____

6. _____

8-11 Preferencias. Complete the following questions with the logical food or drink from the list. Then answer each question using **gustar,** as in the **modelo**.

el pan tostado   los huevos   el té   la ensalada   las papas   los camarones   las zanahorias   el café

MODELO   ¿Prefieres **las papas** fritas o al horno?
Me gustan más fritas (al horno). /
No me gustan las papas.

1. ¿Prefieres _____ con crema, con azúcar o solo?

   _____

2. ¿Prefieres _____ con lechuga o espinacas? ¿con mucho tomate? ¿con o sin cebolla?

   _____

3. ¿Prefieres _____ fritos o a la parrilla?

   _____

4. ¿Prefieres _____ helado o caliente?

   _____

5. ¿Prefieres _____ con mantequilla y mermelada o sin nada?

   _____

6. ¿Prefieres _____ fritos o revueltos (*scrambled*)?

   _____

7. ¿Prefieres _____ cocidas (*cooked*) o crudas (*raw*)?

   _____

8-12 ¿Qué le gusta? Jazmín is a vegetarian. She loves all vegetables and she generally likes all desserts, but she finds meat and seafood revolting. Write sentences using **encantar, gustar,** and **dar asco** to say how she feels about the following foods.

MODELO   Le encantan las zanahorias.

1.   2.   3.   4.   5.   6.

7.   8.   9.

1. _____

2. _____

3. _____

4. _____

5. _____

6. _____

7. _____

8. _____

9. _____

8-13 Marco y Cristina. Cristina is very health-conscious, watches her weight, and doesn't eat out much. Marco doesn't worry about his health, he smokes, and spends a lot of money eating out. Write sentences saying whom the following phrases describe.

MODELO   faltar dinero para cenar en restaurantes caros
          A Cristina le falta dinero para cenar en restaurantes caros.

1. molestar mucho el humo en la sección de fumadores

_____

2. no importar el precio de un restaurante

_____

3. doler el estómago (*his stomach*) a veces porque come mucha grasa

_____

4. dar asco los platos con mucha grasa

_____

5. no interesar comer platos sanos (*healthy*)

_____

6. encantar los postres

_____

8-14 Diario. Write a paragraph comparing your tastes in foods when you were little and now. What did you love and find disgusting when you were young? What do you love and find disgusting now? Are there foods that you used to find revolting that you like now or vice versa? Are there any foods that you used to love that you do not like as much now?

_____

_____

_____

_____

_____

_____

_____

_____

¡A escuchar!

8-15 Orden de preferencia. Listen to a person make four statements about the pictured entrees and determine her order of preference for these dishes. Indicate the order of preference by numbering them from 1 for her favorite to 6 for the one she likes the least.

_____   _____   _____   _____   _____   _____

8-16 Un mal restaurante. Listen as a couple discusses a bad experience they are having at a restaurant. Then complete the following sentences according to what you hear.

1. A él no le gusta el _____ que le sirvieron porque contiene

   _____ y no está _____ como lo pidió.

2. Normalmente, a ella le _____ la _____, pero no

   puede tomar la que le sirvieron esta noche. Le falta _____ y es como

   _____ con _____.

3. Parece que al mesero le molesta _____ de los clientes.

4. Al cliente le falta _____ para _____.

5. Al mesero no le importa _____. Le interesa más _____.

6. Parece que al mesero no le interesa _____.

7. A la clienta le molesta _____.

8-17 ¿Y tú? Imagine that you are going to eat out for the first time with a friend who asks you the following questions. Answer each one with a complete sentence in Spanish.

1. _____

2. _____

3. _____

4. _____

5. _____

6. _____

7. _____

Tema 3 En el mercado

8-18 Un puesto en el mercado. Write the names of the indicated fruits and vegetables with the appropriate definite article (**el, la, los, las**).

1. _____

2. _____

3. _____

4. _____

5. _____

6. _____

7. _____   10. _____

8. _____   11. _____

9. _____   12. _____

8-19 ¿A qué se lo pongo? Say whether you are going to put the following in a spinach salad, a fruit salad, or a cup of coffee.

MODELO   cebolla: **Se la voy a poner a la ensalada de espinacas.**

1. fresas: _____

2. espinacas: _____

3. crema: _____

4. huevo: _____

5. tomates: _____

6. uvas: _____

8-20 ¿A quién? Imagine you have some friends that are coming to dinner. He is a diabetic and doesn't eat sugar, and she is a vegetarian and doesn't eat meat, but they both eat everything else. Say whether you can serve the following things to him, to her, or to both of them.

MODELOS   una chuleta de cerdo: **Se la puedo servir a él pero a ella no.**
arroz: **Se lo puedo servir a los dos.**

1. jamón: _____

2. pastel: _____

3. galletas: _____

4. espinacas: _____

5. ejotes: _____

6. flan: _____

8-21 Una fiesta. Answer the following questions about what was happening when you arrived at this party, replacing the italicized direct objects with pronouns.

MODELO   ¿A quién le enseñaba Verónica *un sitio web*?
             Se lo enseñaba a Daniel.

1. ¿Quién le describía *su página web* a Verónica? _____

2. ¿Quién le traía *más papitas* a Cristina? _____

3. ¿A quién le ofrecía Cristina *más pizza*? _____

4. ¿Quién le daba *comida* al gato? _____

5. ¿A quiénes les contaba *chistes* María? _____

6. ¿A quién le iba a dar *el refresco* Guadalupe? _____

8-22 ¿Quién? A customer is talking about her interactions with a server in a restaurant. Which action from each pair did she do and which did the server do? Describe their interactions using indirect object pronouns, as in the **modelo**.

MODELO   pedir el menú / traer el menú
Yo le pedí el menú al mesero y él me lo trajo.

1. recomendar el plato del día / pedir el plato del día

_____

2. hacer preguntas sobre el menú / explicar el menú

_____

3. ofrecer un postre / decir que no quería nada más

_____

4. pedir la cuenta / traer la cuenta

_____

5. dar una tarjeta de crédito / devolver (*to return*) la tarjeta de crédito

_____

8-23 Diario. Write a paragraph describing a meal you had at a restaurant where you received bad service. What did the server (not) do that displeased you?

_____

_____

_____

_____

_____

_____

_____

_____

¡A escuchar!

8-24 ¿Qué hay en la nevera? Listen as a young couple talks about buying groceries. If they mention something that they already have in the refrigerator, place an **X** in the blank next to it. If they mention something not found in the refrigerator, write it down on the shopping list. The first two items you will hear mentioned have already been indicated as an example.

Lista de la compra

camarones

8-25 Respuestas. Listen to the following questions asked by the server or by customers in a restaurant and place an **X** next to the logical response as you say it aloud. Then listen to the correct response.

MODELO You see: _____ Sí, se lo traigo en seguida. _____ Sí, ¿nos lo trae, por favor?
You hear: ¿Les traigo el menú?
You indicate and say: _____ Sí, se lo traigo en seguida. **X** Sí, ¿nos lo trae, por favor?
You hear: Sí, ¿nos lo trae, por favor?

1. _____ Sí, se lo dimos.   _____ Sí, nos lo dieron.

2. _____ Sí, se los recomiendo.   _____ Sí, se la recomiendo.

3. _____ Sí, voy a traérsela ahora.   _____ Sí, me las van a traer.

4. _____ Sí, nos las pedimos.   _____ No, mi amigo se lo pidió.

5. _____ Sí, ¿nos la trae, por favor?   _____ Sí, nos la acaba de dar.

6. _____ Sí, se la di.   _____ Sí, me la acaba de traer.

Tema 4 Una receta

8-26 Indicaciones. Give **Ud.** commands saying what to do with the following foods.

MODELO   **Derrita la mantequilla.**   derretir

1. calentar   2. agregarle a la sopa   3. batir   4. mezclar

1. _____

2. _____

3. _____

4. _____

8-27 Una sopa de verduras. You are explaining to someone how to make vegetable soup. Tell him whether to add the following ingredients?

MODELO   plátanos: **No, no los agregue.**
           tomates: **Sí, agréguelos.**

1. chícharos: _____

2. piña: _____

3. sal y pimienta: _____

4. fresas: _____

5. maíz: _____

6. queso suizo: _____

8-28 Consejos. Give a group of people good advice about health by telling them to make one of the choices listed, and not to do the other. Use **Uds.** commands.

MODELO   utilizar muchos productos procesados / comprar frutas y verduras frescas
           No utilicen muchos productos procesados. Compren frutas y verduras frescas.

1. desayunar todas las mañanas / cenar muy tarde

_____

2. fumar / dejar de (*stop*) fumar

_____

3. dormir lo suficiente (*enough*) / acostarse muy tarde

_____

4. tomar mucha cerveza / evitar (*to avoid*) el alcohol

_____

5. comer mucha carne roja / pedir pescado o pollo

_____

6. salir todos los días a restaurantes / preparar comida sana (*healthy*) en casa

_____

7. hacer ejercicio con regularidad / ser perezosos

_____

8. ir al médico si están enfermos / venir a clase enfermos

_____

8-29 Consejos. Imagine that you are a counselor for people suffering from depression. Would you tell someone to do or not to do the following things in order to stay happy and healthy? Fill in the blanks logically with affirmative or negative **Ud.** commands of the verbs in parentheses. Then in the blanks on the right, rank the different pieces of advice from 1 to 14, with 1 for the advice you consider the most valuable and 14 the least.

1. _____ (dedicar) tiempo a la meditación.   _____

2. _____ (dedicar) todo su tiempo al trabajo.   _____

3. _____ (ser) impaciente.   _____

4. _____ (insistir) en siempre tener razón.   _____

5. _____ (seguir) una rutina.   _____

6. _____ (acostarse) a horas diferentes cada día.   _____

7. _____ (perder) el contacto con la naturaleza (*nature*).   _____

8. _____ (tener) un perro o un gato.   _____

9. _____ (pensar) en los problemas del pasado.   _____

10. _____ (divertirse) con los amigos con frecuencia.   _____

11. _____ (organizar) su tiempo efectivamente.   _____

12. _____ (tener) un pasatiempo.   _____

13. _____ (hacer) la misma comida todos los días.   _____

14. _____ (ir) de vacaciones a un lugar nuevo.   _____

8-30 Cortesía. You can often change a command (**Tráigame..., por favor.** *Bring me... please.*) to a more polite sounding request by simply making a question with the present tense form of the verb (**¿Me trae..., por favor?** *Would you please bring me...?*). Answer the following questions a server asks with the logical response from the list, changing the command to a request.

Prepáremelo término medio, por favor.   Tráigame la cuenta, por favor.
Sírvamela ahora, por favor.   Deme el brócoli y las espinacas, por favor.
Tráigame un agua mineral, por favor.   Sí, explíqueme qué hay en el mole, por favor.

Modelo   ¿Qué quisiera tomar?
            ¿Me trae un agua mineral, por favor?

1. ¿Tiene preguntas sobre el menú? _____

2. ¿Cómo quiere el bistec? _____

3. ¿Qué verduras quiere con eso? _____

4. ¿Le sirvo la ensalada ahora o más tarde? _____

5. ¿Le puedo ofrecer algo más esta noche? _____

8-31 Diario. Imagine that you are explaining to a group of people how to make your favorite dish. List the ingredients that you need and then explain the preparation using **Uds.** commands. If you do not know how to cook, search the web for **recetas** and pick one to explain. You may have to look up a few words in a dictionary to explain your recipe.

_____

_____

_____

_____

_____

_____

¡A escuchar!

8-32 Receta de galletas de choco-chip. Listen to the following recipe for chocolate chip cookies and fill in the missing ingredients and instructions.

Ingredientes:

1 _____ derretida   1 _____

¾ de _____ blanco   2 _____

½ de _____ moreno

1½ taza de confi-chips de _____

2¼ _____

1 cucharadita de polvo de hornear (*baking powder*)

½ cucharadita de _____

Preparación:

1. En _____, _____ la mantequilla, los azúcares, la vainilla y los huevos.

2. _____, el polvo de hornear y _____.

3. _____ hasta formar una pasta.

4. _____ los confi-chips de _____.

5. Forme bolitas aplastadas (*flattened balls*) y _____ en una charola de horno (*baking tray*) engrasada y enharinada.

6. _____ el horno a 190°C.

7. _____ en el horno de ocho a diez minutos.

8-33 El señor o la señora Modales. Imagine that you give advice on proper etiquette on a radio show. Write an answer to each question you hear with an **Ud.** command, replacing the direct object with a pronoun.

1. _____

2. _____

3. _____

4. _____

Tema 5 Una dieta

8-34 ¿Me los recomiendas? Would a health-conscious person recommend the following foods and drinks to a friend? Complete the following sentences using direct and indirect object pronouns in the first blank and the logical item in parentheses to explain why.

MODELO   la cerveza (mucho alcohol, mucha grasa)
No, no te la recomiendo porque contiene **mucho alcohol.**

1. el helado (mucha grasa, mucha vitamina C)

_____ porque contiene _____.

2. las zanahorias (mucha vitamina A, mucha cafeína)

_____ porque contienen _____.

3. el café (mucha cafeína, muchas proteínas)

_____ porque contiene _____.

4. las espinacas (varias vitaminas, mucho azúcar)

_____ porque contienen _____.

5. los refrescos (mucho azúcar, mucha sal)

_____ porque contienen _____.

6. los cereales (mucha fibra, mucha grasa)

_____ porque contienen _____.

8-35 Repite, por favor. Give the same advice as in the preceding activity, using **tú** commands with the verb **tomar** or **comer** to tell a friend whether to drink or eat each item frequently.

MODELO   la cerveza (mucho alcohol, mucha grasa)
No la tomes con frecuencia porque contiene **mucho alcohol.**

1. _____ con frecuencia porque contiene _____.

2. _____ con frecuencia porque contienen _____.

3. _____ con frecuencia porque contiene _____.

4. _____ con frecuencia porque contienen _____.

5. _____ con frecuencia porque contienen _____.

6. _____ con frecuencia porque contienen _____.

8-36 Mandatos. Complete the following chart with the missing commands. The first one has been done as an example.

	Tú Affirmative	Tú Negative	Ud. All Commands	Uds. All Commands
1.	*deja*	*no dejes*	*(no) deje*	(no) dejen
2.	evita			
3.			(no) tome	
4.				(no) empiecen
5.		no comas		
6.			(no) pierda	
7.		no seas		
8.				(no) hagan
9.		no vayas		
10.	sal			

Now use the appropriate command from the chart to do the following.

MODELO   *tell a friend to stop smoking*
               Deja de fumar.

1. *tell a group of people to begin the day with exercise*

_____

2. *tell a friend not to be lazy*

_____

3. *tell a friend to exercise with you*

_____

4. *tell a group of people to avoid alcohol and caffeine*

_____

5. *tell a group of people not to lose patience (**la paciencia**)*

_____

6. *tell a friend to go to the gym with you*

_____

8-37 Consejos. Which advice from the list might you give a friend or classmate who says the following things to you? Use **tú** commands in your responses.

ponerse un suéter   no salir con los amigos todas las noches
salir más temprano de casa   traer algo para comer entre las clases
ir a ver al profesor a su oficina   venir conmigo a la biblioteca

MODELO   Siempre estoy cansada en mis clases.
               Pues (*Well*), **¡no salgas con los amigos todas las noches!**

1. Siempre llego tarde a mi primera clase.

   Pues, ¡_____!

2. Siempre tengo frío en mis clases.

   Pues, ¡_____!

3. También tengo hambre en mi segunda clase.

   Pues, ¡_____!

4. No entiendo nada en mi clase de física.

   Pues, ¡_____!

5. ¿Me puedes ayudar a estudiar para el examen?

   Sí, cómo no, ¡_____!

8-38 Diario. Imagine that your conscience is telling you what (not) to do to improve your life. Write at least three commands it might give you of what to do and three commands of what not to do to be happy and healthy. Give a brief explanation why you should (not) do each one.

_____

_____

_____

_____

_____

_____

_____

_____

¡A escuchar!

8-39 Tú también. Someone is giving advice to **el Sr. Morales**. Use **tú** form commands to tell his son **Benjamín** to do or not to do the same things. Then, as you hear the correct response, write the command in the blank.

MODELO   You hear: Coma Ud. más verduras.
              You say: **Tú también, Benjamín, come más verduras.**
              You hear: Tú también, Benjamín, come más verduras.
              You write: Tú también, Benjamín, **come más verduras.**

1. Tú también, Benjamín, _____.

2. Tú también, Benjamín, _____.

3. Tú también, Benjamín, _____.

4. Tú también, Benjamín, _____.

5. Tú también, Benjamín, _____.

6. Tú también, Benjamín, _____.

7. Tú también, Benjamín, _____.

8-40 Recomendaciones. A friend is asking for advice. Respond to each statement that you hear with the logical response from each pair, putting the verb in the command form for **tú**. Then, as you hear the correct response, write the verb form in the logical answer.

MODELO   You see: _____ (no cenar) tan tarde. / _____
                           (no cenar) muy temprano.
              You hear: A veces no duermo bien por la noche porque tengo indigestión.
              You answer: **No cenes tan tarde.**
              You hear: No cenes tan tarde.
              You write: _____**No cenes**_____ (no cenar) tan tarde. / _____
                           (no cenar) muy temprano.

1. _____ (no ir) al gimnasio. / _____ (venir) conmigo al gimnasio.

2. _____ (no ir) a los bufetes. / _____ (comer) más fuerte a mediodía.

3. _____ (dejar) de fumar. / _____ (evitar) los platos con mucha grasa.

4. _____ (levantarse) más temprano. / _____ (acostarse) un rato.

5. _____ (salir) con ellos. / _____ (no salir) con ellos.

¡Trato hecho!

8-41 En la red. One aspect of foreign cultures that nearly everyone finds interesting is food! Look on the Web for recipes from a Spanish-speaking region by searching for *recetas mexicanas (cubanas, puertorriqueñas, españolas, argentinas, colombianas, guatemaltecas...)* to find recipes from the region you wish to explore. Write the addresses of interesting sites that you find and answer the questions that follow.

www._____

www._____

www._____

1. Find an interesting recipe in Spanish for each of the following types of dishes. Write the name of the dish in Spanish, then briefly explain what it is in English.

una ensalada: _____

_____

una sopa: _____

_____

un plato principal: _____

_____

un postre: _____

_____

2. Pick one of the recipes listed above, and explain to a friend—in English—how to prepare it. Indicate which Web site it is from at the top of your explanation.

www._____

_____

_____

_____

_____

_____

8-42 Composición. Do you eat a balanced diet? Do you lead a healthy life? Write three paragraphs that describe your eating habits and lifestyle. In the first paragraph, describe your typical diet. Do you eat enough fruits and vegetables? Do you eat too much of something? In the second paragraph, describe what you ate for breakfast, lunch, and dinner yesterday. Finally, in the third paragraph, mention other aspects of your lifestyle that lead to good health or that you need to change. For example, do you smoke? Do you avoid alcohol? Do you have a lot of stress because you are disorganized? You may incorporate anything that you wrote in your **Diarios**.

_____

_____

_____

_____

_____

_____

_____

_____

_____

_____

_____

_____

_____

_____

_____

_____

_____

Nombre: _____   Fecha: _____

9   Con el médico

Tema 1 ¿Te lastimaste?

9-1 El cuerpo. Write the names of the different parts of the body shown on the illustration.

1._____ 8._____

2._____ 9._____

3._____ 10._____

4._____ 11._____

5._____ 12._____

6._____ 13._____

7._____ 14._____

15._____

16._____

17._____

9-2 ¡Cuidado! Which thing from each pair would you tell a friend to do, and which one would you tell him/her not to do?

MODELO   tener cuidado (*to be careful*) / cortarse el dedo con el cuchillo
Ten cuidado. No te cortes el dedo con el cuchillo.

1. tener cuidado / caerse de la escalera: _____

2. ponerse nerviosa por el examen / relajarse: _____

3. resfriarse / ponerse un suéter: _____

Capítulo 9 • Con el médico   177

4. quemarse la espalda con el sol / ponerse crema protectora: _____

_____

5. levantarse con cuidado / darse un golpe contra la mesa: _____

_____

6. ponerse zapatos buenos / torcerse el tobillo durante la carrera (race): _____

_____

9-3 ¡Cuídense! Tell the following people to do or not to do the logical thing from the list below, according to each illustration. Use a **tú** command if one person is pictured and **ustedes** for two. Then write a second statement saying how they are going to hurt themselves otherwise, using a verb presented on page 264 of the textbook with a logical part of the body.

no usar zapatos de tacón (*heel*) tan alto   ponerse crema protectora solar

no ir tan rápido con la bicicleta   tener más cuidado con el cuchillo   no jugar cerca de la mesa

no ser tan impaciente con la comida   no correr tan rápido con el caballo

MODELO   **¡No vayas tan rápido con la bicicleta! ¡Te vas a caer y romper el brazo!**

1.   2.   3.

4.   5.   6.

1. _____

2. _____

3. _____

4. _____

5. _____

6. _____

9-4 ¿Te duele mucho? Complete the following conversation in which a person tells his friend about an accident that he had with words from the list. Some words may be used twice. Conjugate the verbs in the preterite or present tense as necessary.

muletas	resfriarse	enyesada	doler	lastimarse	quitar	caerse	vendado	pasar

— Carlos, ¿qué te (1) _____? ¿Cómo (2) _____?

— Hola, Graciela. No fue nada grave, (3) _____ de la bicicleta.

— ¿Nada grave? ¡Tienes el brazo (4) _____, y la pierna

(5) _____! ¿Te (6) _____ mucho?

— El brazo, no. Pero la pierna me (7) _____ bastante. Y estoy un poco cansado

de andar con (8) _____.

— Y ¿cuándo te van a (9) _____ el yeso?

— No lo sé. Y tú, ¿cómo estás?

— Ahora mejor. La semana pasada (10) _____ y estuve en la cama todo el fin de

semana con una tos terrible.

— Bueno, cuídate, Graciela.

— Sí, tú también, Carlos.

9-5 Diario. Write a paragraph describing an accident that you had. Describe the circumstances in which the accident occurred. Use the names of the different parts of the body and the preterite or the imperfect of the reflexive verbs that you learned in this **Tema**.

_____

_____

_____

_____

_____

_____

_____

_____

¡A escuchar!

9-6 ¿Qué te pasó? Listen and complete the following conversation in which Héctor tells his classmate Noelia about an accident he had while riding a horse. Pay special attention to the reflexive verbs that you learned in this **Tema**.

— Héctor, ¿qué te pasó? ¿(1) _____?

— Sí, Noelia, (2) _____ a caballo, y (3) _____.

— ¿(4) _____ el brazo?

— Sí, y también (5) _____ el tobillo.

— Oh, pobrecito, y ¿(6) _____ mucho?

— Ahora no tanto, pero cuando (7) _____ el golpe...

— ¿Cuándo te (8) _____ el yeso?

— Dentro de tres semanas.

— Ay, qué mala suerte.

— Y tú, Noelia, ¿sigues (9) _____ por lo de tu novio?

— (10) _____, no vale la pena (*it's not worth it*) preocuparse por alguien como él.

9-7 Advertencias. Listen to the warnings a teacher gives to students in her kindergarten class and complete the first blank of each sentence with the part of the body that you hear. Then give the same warning in the form of a negative command. Listen and repeat as you hear the correct warning, and write it in the second blank.

MODELO   You see: Pepe, te vas a cortar _____. ¡_____!
You hear: Pepe, te vas a cortar los dedos.
You write: Pepe, te vas a cortar **los dedos.**
You say: **¡No te cortes los dedos!**
You hear: ¡No te cortes los dedos!
You write: Pepe, te vas a cortar **los dedos. ¡No te cortes los dedos!**

1. Beatriz, te vas a lastimar _____. ¡_____!

2. Juan, Carlos, se van a poner malos del _____. ¡_____!

3. Julia, te vas a quemar _____. ¡_____!

4. Sara, Pedro, se van a torcer _____. ¡_____!

5. Enrique, te vas a dar un golpe en _____. ¡_____!

6. Lola, Carla, se van caer de _____. ¡_____!

Tema 2 ¡Cuídense!

9-8 En la clase de salud. Complete the following conversation that a teacher is having with her students during a health lesson with the logical words from the list.

sistema inmunológico	ejercicio	estirarse	cuidar	atún	vitaminas
alimentos	prevenir	ricos	mantenerse		

— ¿Qué necesitan hacer ustedes para (1) _____ la salud y para

(2) _____ en forma?

— Necesitamos comer (3) _____ sanos y hacer

(4) _____.

— ¿Es bueno comer pescados como el (5) _____ y el salmón?

— Sí, porque son (6) _____ en hierro (*iron*).

— ¿Es bueno comer frutas?

— Sí, porque tienen muchas (7) _____ y son buenas para el

(8) _____.

— Cuando hacen ejercicio, ¿es bueno (9) _____ antes?

— Sí, para (10) _____ accidentes serios cuando hacemos deporte.

9-9 A dieta. Using a **nosotros** command, suggest to some friends whether or not to do the following things if you want to improve your health.

MODELO   salir a un restaurante de comida rápida
No salgamos a un restaurante de comida rápida.

1. ir al gimnasio cada mañana a las siete

_____

2. seguir una dieta sana y equilibrada para bajar de peso

_____

3. desayunar fuerte y cenar ligero

_____

4. hacer platos bajos en calorías

_____

5. ponerles mucha sal a las comidas

_____

6. tener cuidado con los productos ricos en grasa

_____

7. dormir todo el tiempo

_____

8. dar un paseo (*go for a walk*) después de cada comida

_____

9-10 Estados y resultados. Imagine that your friends say the following things to you. Give a logical **nosotros** command with an item from the list.

ir en bicicleta	**tomar un agua mineral**	**pedir una ensalada de fruta**
ponerse crema protectora	**estirarse antes de jugar**	**dormir una siesta**

MODELO   Jugamos el partido dentro de media hora. **Estirémonos antes de jugar.**

1. Estamos muy cansados. _____

2. Nos quemamos muy fácilmente con el sol. _____

3. Tenemos mucha sed. _____

4. Estamos a dieta y no comemos dulces. _____

5. Hace un día muy bueno para ir al parque. _____

9-11 Una dieta equilibrada. Make a **nosotros** command with the indicated verb and one of the items pictured, according to the context.

MODELO   no pedir: **No pidamos pizza.**
            Contiene mucha grasa. No es buena para el corazón.

1. no tomar demasiada...: _____
   Contiene alcohol y no es buena para el sistema inmunológico.

2. comer: _____
   Contiene muchas proteínas que son necesarias para tener los músculos fuertes.

3. evitar usar demasiada...: _____
   Contiene mucho colesterol y grasa y no es buena para el corazón.

4. preparar...: _____
   Contienen vitamina A y son buenas para la piel y los ojos.

5. no hacer: _____
   Contiene azúcar y soy diabético.

6. servir: _____
   Contienen vitamina C, que es importante para prevenir problemas respiratorios.

9-12 ¿Y tú? Answer these questions that a friend might ask you regarding your eating and exercise habits with complete sentences in Spanish.

1. ¿Qué haces para mantenerte en buena forma?

   _____

2. ¿Sigues una dieta equilibrada? ¿Qué alimentos forman parte de tu dieta?

   _____

3. ¿Cómo te cuidas para no ponerte enfermo?

   _____

4. ¿Qué te produce estrés? ¿Qué haces para relajarte?

   _____

9-13 Diario. In two paragraphs, describe ideal health habits, first in terms of diet, then concerning exercise and stress control. Incorporate the vocabulary that you learned in this **Tema** and use infinitives after structures to express necessity, such as **es necesario**, **es importante**, **se necesita**, or **se debe**.

_____

_____

_____

_____

_____

_____

¡A escuchar!

9-14 En la clínica _A la medida_. Listen to this radio commercial about a weight loss clinic and complete the ad with the words that you hear.

Ya llegan las vacaciones de verano: la playa, los trajes de baño... el estrés de la báscula (*scales*). ¿Se siente

(1) _____? ¿Siente (2) _____? En la clínica _A la_

medida tenemos la solución a sus problemas; le podemos (3) _____ a perder esos

kilos de más tan molestos que ganó durante el invierno. Si quiere (4) _____

llámenos hoy o venga a visitarnos a uno de nuestros establecimientos oficiales que

(5) _____ por todo el condado de Carreño. En la clínica _A la medida_ creamos

una (6) _____ individualizada y (7) _____ para cada

cliente y le ayudamos a (8) _____ el peso adecuado. Nosotros sabemos cómo

(9) _____ de usted. Póngase en nuestras (10) _____.

9-15 Una vida sana. Imagine that a friend is asking you each question that you hear and suggest that you do the healthier option using a **nosotros** command. You will then hear the correct answer. Repeat it and write your suggestion in the blank provided.

MODELO	You hear:	¿Prefieres servir refrescos o agua mineral con la comida?
	You say:	**Sirvamos agua mineral.**
	You hear:	Sirvamos agua mineral.
	You repeat and write:	**Sirvamos agua mineral.**

1. _____

2. _____

3. _____

4. _____

5. _____

6. _____

7. _____

8. _____

9. _____

10. _____

Tema 3 ¿Qué síntomas tiene?

9-16 ¿Qué les duele? Look at the illustrations and select one of the phrases from the list to describe each person´s symptoms. Put the verbs in the **él/ella** form.

sentirse mareado   estornudar   dolerle el oído   tener catarro   picarle el ojo
tener fiebre   necesitar una curita   tener el dedo hinchado

1.   2.   3.   4.

5.   6.   7.    8.

1. _____

2. _____

3. _____

4. _____

5. _____

6. _____

7. _____

8. _____

9-17 No me siento bien, doctor. Imagine a conversation between the patient and the doctor in the illustration. Incorporate the structures to describe symptoms that you learned in this **Tema**.

— _____

— _____

— _____

— _____

— _____

— _____

— _____

— _____

9-18 Recomendaciones. Select the logical recommendation from the options provided in parentheses to attend each patient's need. Conjugate the verbs in the subjunctive.

1. Tengo mucha fiebre. El médico me recomienda que _____.

   _____ (hacer ejercicio / guardar cama)

2. A mi madre le duele mucho el estómago. Los médicos le prohíben que _____.

   _____ (comer sopas / comer comidas muy picantes [*hot, spicy*])

3. Mis hermanos tienen alergias en la primavera. Su médica les sugiere que _____.

   _____ (no hacer muchas actividades al aire libre / salir al campo a pasear)

4. Mis amigos y yo tenemos mucho estrés. El profesor quiere que _____.

   _____ (organizar mejor nuestro tiempo / salir todas las noches a los bares)

5. Tú tienes el tobillo hinchado. El médico te recomienda que _____.

   _____ (correr cinco millas cada día / no jugar al fútbol por unas semanas)

6. Mis padres y yo estamos resfriados. Nuestra doctora insiste en que _____.

   _____ (tomar más vitaminas / ponerse una curita)

9-19 Preferencias. Complete the following sentences logically with endings from the list. In each case decide whether to use the subjunctive or the infinitive.

sentirse mejor pronto   comer mucha grasa
fumar en las habitaciones   no tener muchas visitas
ser individuales   hacer ejercicio
ver a un médico   cuidar a los pacientes

1. Mi médico no quiere que yo _____.

2. Los pacientes prefieren que las habitaciones _____.

3. El enfermero insiste en que el enfermo _____.

4. Necesito urgentemente _____.

5. La doctora nos recomienda que _____.

6. El enfermo espera _____.

7. El hospital prohíbe que los pacientes _____.

8. Los médicos y las enfermeras necesitan _____.

9-20 Diario. Write a paragraph about how often you get sick. Do you have allergies? Do you catch a cold easily? Do you get hurt often? What are the symptoms? What does the doctor recommend to you in each situation?

_____

_____

_____

_____

_____

_____

_____

_____

_____

_____

_____

¡A escuchar!

9-21 ¿Qué síntomas tiene? Listen to the following conversations between Dr. Losada and his patients and complete the dialogues with the words describing the patient's symptoms and the doctor's advice that you hear.

A. — Buenos días, señora Arias. ¿No se siente bien?

— No, doctor Losada, (1) _____ y

(2) _____.

— Sí, también (3) _____. Le recomiendo que

(4) _____ y descanse.

B. — Hola, Miguelito. ¿Cómo estás?

— Estoy enfermo, doctor. (5) _____ y

(6) _____.

— Déjame (7) _____. Sí, tienes un poco de

infección. Te voy a (8) _____ un antibiótico. Espero que

(9) _____ mejor pronto.

C. — Buenas tardes, señor García. ¿Cómo está?

— No muy bien. (10) _____ y (11) _____.

— Parece que tiene una (12) _____ muy fuerte y necesita tomar

(13) _____. Le aconsejo que no (14) _____ de

casa en varios días.

9-22 ¿Se cuida? Imagine that you have the flu and a doctor is asking you the following questions. Answer each one with a complete sentence in Spanish.

1. _____

2. _____

3. _____

4. _____

5. _____

6. _____

Tema 4 ¿Quiere vivir 100 años?

9-23 Consejos para una vida más larga. Give advice for living a longer life by saying whether or not to do the following things. Use **Uds.** commands.

MODELO   mantener una dieta equilibrada: **Mantengan una dieta equilibrada.**

1. trabajar más todo el tiempo: _____

2. manejar con cuidado: _____

3. ir al médico una vez al año: _____

4. tomar el sol con moderación: _____

5. llevar una vida con estrés: _____

6. subir de peso: _____

7. consumir muchas bebidas alcohólicas: _____

8. hacer ejercicio con regularidad: _____

9. estirarse antes de hacer ejercicio: _____

10. tomar comidas con mucha sal: _____

11. mantenerse en contacto con la naturaleza: _____

12. tener siempre tiempo para relajarse: _____

9-24 En caso de infarto. Complete the following suggestions of how to prevent heart attacks and what to do to assist a heart attack victim with verbs from the list. Conjugate the verbs as **Ud.** commands as necessary.

| tener | insistir | prevenir | abusar | ponerse | tratar | prohibir |

El infarto es común en las personas con presión arterial alta. (1) _____ el infarto

y sus consecuencias negativas con una dieta equilibrada y haciendo ejercicio con regularidad.

(2) _____ en su dieta alimentos integrales y no

(3) _____ de las comidas ricas en grasa, ni del alcohol. Si debe ayudar a una

víctima de un infarto, primero no (4) _____ nervioso y llame a una ambulancia.

(5) _____ en que el paciente no se mueva, y (6) _____

de calmarlo. (7) _____ al enfermo que se levante o camine hasta que llegue el

médico.

9-25 Es una lástima... Complete the following conversations with the logical expression from those given in parentheses. Conjugate the verbs in the subjunctive form, as necessary.

A. — Raquel, tienes mala cara. ¿Qué te pasa?

— No sé, pero duermo mal y tengo muchos dolores de cabeza.

— Ay, chica, (es común / más vale) (1) _____ que (ir al médico / volver a la

oficina) (2) _____.

B. — Hola, Profesora Sánchez. ¿No se siente bien?

— La verdad es que no. Tengo alergias y estornudo todo el tiempo.

— Lo siento mucho. (Ojalá / Es raro) (3) _____ que (tener clase mañana /

sentirse mejor pronto) (4) _____.

C. — Hola, mamá. ¿Cómo estás?

— Regular, hija. Me torcí el tobillo mientras corría por el parque y me duele mucho.

— Oh, no. (Es una lástima / Es preferible) (5) _____ que (hacer ejercicio / ir

al médico) (6) _____.

D. — Teresa, David, los veo un poco cansados. ¿Qué tal su viaje?

— No muy bien. Teresa se puso enferma del estómago y vomitaba todo el tiempo.

— ¿En serio? La verdad es que (es común / es ridículo) (7) _____ que un

turista (enfermarse / divertirse) (8) _____ cuando viaja a un país

extranjero.

E. — Jorge, te veo un poco triste.

— Sí, desde que perdí mi empleo me siento muy mal y no tengo ganas de hacer nada.

— Escucha, (es urgente / es normal) (9) _____ que (estar deprimido / tener

razón) (10) _____.

9-26 Reacciones. React to the following statements with one of the expressions from the list and any logical ending of your choice with a verb in the subjunctive.

Es increíble que	Más vale que	Es urgente que	Es normal que	Es mejor que	Ojalá que

MODELO   El consumo de tabaco entre los adolescentes es muy alto.
Es mejor que los adolescentes no fumen.

1. Muchos niños en nuestra sociedad actual desarrollan malos hábitos alimenticios en el colegio.

   _____

2. Muchos profesionales de hoy tienen mucho estrés y sufren de depresión.

   _____

3. Muchos niños pasan demasiado tiempo sentados en frente del televisor.

   _____

4. Las personas con presión arterial alta tienen más riesgo (*risk*) de sufrir un infarto.

   _____

5. Muchos inmigrantes en Estados Unidos no tienen seguro médico.

   _____

9-27 Diario. Do you agree with the statements mentioned in the preceding activity? Select one of them and write a paragraph making subjective comments on the negative consequences of the problem and how to address it.

_____

_____

_____

_____

_____

_____

_____

¡A escuchar!

9-28 Consejos. Listen to friends describe their problems and write the number of each statement in the blank with the logical advice you might give, reading the advice aloud. Then listen and repeat, checking your work as you hear the correct answer.

MODELO   You hear: Me corté el dedo con el cuchillo preparando la comida.
You say: **Más vale que te pongas una curita.** *and you write the number of the question next to it.*
You hear: Más vale que te pongas una curita.
You repeat: **Más vale que te pongas una curita.**

a. _____ Más vale que te calientes cerca de la estufa.

b. _____ Es importante que dejes de fumar.

c. _____ Recomiendo que busques otro trabajo.

d. **Modelo** Más vale que te pongas una curita.

e. _____ Más vale que te estires antes de hacer ejercicio.

f. _____ Recomiendo que llames una ambulancia y que te acuestes.

9-29 Es bueno que... Listen to the following comments that friends make about their eating and exercise habits, and comment accordingly as in the model. Then repeat as you hear the correct answer and fill in the blank with the missing words.

MODELO   You see: Es bueno que siempre _____.
You hear: Siempre duermo ocho horas.
You say: **Es bueno que siempre duermas ocho horas.**
You hear: Es bueno que siempre duermas ocho horas.
You repeat: **Es bueno que siempre duermas ocho horas.**
You write: Es bueno que siempre **duermas ocho horas.**

1. Es bueno que _____ en frutas y verduras.

2. Es importante que _____ en la playa.

3. Es necesario que _____ un chequeo médico una vez al año.

4. Es mejor que _____.

5. Es preferible que generalmente _____.

6. Más vale que nunca _____.

Tema 5 La dieta y las enfermedades

9-30 Sufre de... Indicate the health problem associated with the following symptoms. Use the expression **sufrir de** in your responses.

| fiebre del heno | insomnio | artritis | diabetes | congestión |

MODELO   Mi esposa se pone muy nerviosa por las noches y no puede dormir.
Sufre de insomnio.

1. Me duelen los pulmones. No respiro bien y toso con frecuencia.

   _____

2. A mis abuelos les duelen mucho los huesos de las manos, las piernas y la espalda.

   _____

3. Mi hijo estornuda mucho y tiene la nariz siempre tapada. _____

4. Mi esposo pierde peso sin razón. _____

9-31 Definiciones. Which parts of the body do these definitions describe? Write the logical words from the list.

| los huesos | el corazón | los riñones | la sangre |
| el estómago | el páncreas | los pulmones | el cerebro |

1. _____ es un líquido rojo que circula por las venas y las arterias.

2. _____ es el músculo necesario para la circulación de la sangre.

3. _____ forman el esqueleto de los animales vertebrados.

4. _____ son los órganos principales de la respiración.

5. _____ es el centro del sistema nervioso situado en el cráneo.

6. _____ son los órganos principales del tracto urinario.

7. _____ es el órgano donde empieza la digestión.

8. _____ es la glándula situada detrás del estómago que produce insulina, la hormona que limita la cantidad de glucosa en la sangre.

Now indicate which item from the list at the top of the activity you associate with each of the following conditions.

1. la pulmonía: _____

5. la alta presión arterial: _____

2. la diabetes: _____

6. una infección urinaria: _____

3. un infarto: _____

7. una úlcera: _____

4. la osteoporosis: _____

9-32 Dudo que... Express your uncertainty, doubt, or disagreement concerning the following statements related to health habits, using the following expressions with the subjunctive.

| No es cierto que | Es improbable que | Dudo que | No es verdad que |
| No creo que | No estoy seguro/a de que | | Es imposible que |

MODELO   Los alimentos con mucha grasa ayudan a bajar el colesterol.
No es cierto que los alimentos con mucha grasa ayuden a bajar el colesterol.

1. Hacer ejercicio con regularidad produce insomnio.

_____.

2. El chocolate previene la diabetes.

_____.

3. El dolor de cabeza es un síntoma del infarto.

_____.

4. Beber mucho café previene la artritis.

_____.

5. Consumir mucha carne ayuda el sistema inmunológico.

_____.

9-33 En la consulta.   Complete the following conversation between a patient and his doctor with the appropriate word from the list below. Conjugate the verbs as necessary.

| garganta | ser | pulmones | grados | alérgico | tos | guardar |
| sentirse | cuidarse | síntomas | recetar | penicilina | | volver |

— Buenos días, Gonzalo. ¿Cómo está?

— (1) _____ muy mal, doctor Álvarez. Quizás sea gripe.

— Es posible. Dígame, ¿qué (2) _____ tiene?

— Me duele la (3) _____, tengo (4) _____ y no puedo dormir por las noches.

— Sí, tiene los (5) _____ muy congestionados con 40

(6) _____ de temperatura.

— ¿Qué me puede (7) _____, doctor?

— ¿Es usted (8) _____ a algo?

— Sí, soy alérgico a la (9) _____.

— Bueno, le voy a recetar unas pastillas. No creo que (10) _____ nada grave,

pero quiero que (11) _____ mucho y (12) _____

cama. Dudo que (13) _____ al trabajo esta semana.

9-34 Es posible que... Say what illness might cause the following symptoms, as in the **modelo**.

MODELO   Si tienes mucha tos y te duele el pecho, **es posible que tengas pulmonía.**

1. Si estornudas con frecuencia y te pican los ojos, _____

_____.

2. Si sientes que no vales nada y no quieres salir ni divertirte, _____

_____.

3. Si tienes dolor muscular y te duelen los oídos y la garganta, _____

_____.

9-35 Diario. What do you do when you feel sick? Do you go to the doctor right away? Do you prefer to use home remedies for some of your health problems? Do you think that herbs and home remedies are as effective as prescription medicines? Describe your beliefs about healthcare.

_____

_____

_____

_____

_____

_____

_____

¡A escuchar!

9-36 ¿De qué sufren? Listen to the following symptoms and complete the sentences you see with the logical ending from those in parentheses. Then listen and repeat as you hear the correct answer, and fill in the blank with missing words.

MODELO   You see: Es posible que Arturo _____.
(tener artritis / sufrir de fiebre del heno)
You hear: Arturo estornuda mucho y no respira bien.
You say: **Es posible que Arturo sufra de fiebre del heno.**
You hear: Es posible que Arturo sufra de fiebre del heno.
You repeat: **Es posible que Arturo sufra de fiebre del heno.**
You write: Es posible que Arturo **sufra de fiebre del heno**.

1. Es posible que _____. (tener el brazo roto / sufrir de insomnio)

2. Dudo que _____. (ir al trabajo hoy / guardar cama)

3. Es posible que _____. (tener diabetes / comer demasiado)

4. Quizás _____. (ser artritis / ser un infarto)

5. Es probable que _____. (sufrir de artritis / sufrir de fiebre del heno)

6. Dudo que _____. (ser grave / toser)

7. Quizás _____. (sufrir de depresión / tener la pierna rota)

8. Tal vez _____. (tener un catarro / estar roto)

9-37 ¿Estás segura? Listen to a conversation between two friends who talk about Natalia's boyfriend, Andrés, who is very sick. Complete the dialogue with the words that you hear.

— Natalia, ¿cómo estás? Te veo preocupada.

— Sí, mi novio está muy enfermo, yo creo que (1) _____.

— ¿Estás segura de que (2) _____? Eso es muy grave.

— Sí, tiene los pulmones muy congestionados y no puede respirar.

— Bueno, mujer, es posible que sólo (3) _____.

— No sé, creo que debe (4) _____.

— Natalia, dudo que Andrés (5) _____. Es tan activo... y además nunca está enfermo.

— Estoy segura de que no (6) _____ últimamente. Trabaja demasiado y no es

verdad que (7) _____ lo suficiente, como él dice.

— Es posible que (8) _____; debes pedirle que vaya al médico.

— No creo que me (9) _____, pero voy a tratar de ayudarlo.

¡Trato hecho!

9-38 En la red. Search the Web in Spanish for the different kinds of diets available on the market that promise miracle results to the people concerned about their weight. Begin by searching for *dietas* and *populares*. Check the sites you find for the information requested below and answer the questions in Spanish. Write down the addresses of the interesting and useful sites you discover and share them with your instructor and other students.

Addresses of useful and interesting sites:

www._____

www._____

www._____

1. ¿Cuáles son dos de las dietas más populares ahora?

   _____

   _____

   _____

2. ¿Cuáles son algunos de los supuestos beneficios de estas dietas?

   _____

   _____

   _____

   _____

   _____

3. ¿Tiene Ud. dudas sobre estas dietas o le parecen buenas? ¿Por qué?

   _____

   _____

   _____

   _____

   _____

   _____

9-39 Composición. Combining what you wrote in your **Diarios** and adding additional details, write a composition describing your feelings about the healthcare that you receive. In the first paragraph, talk about how often you are ill, what types of illnesses you most commonly have, and whether you go to the doctor. In the second paragraph, describe the last time you went to the doctor. What were your symptoms and what did the doctor do to help you? Finally, discuss your feelings about the healthcare that you receive and the healthcare system in general. Is it good? Are there any changes that you think are needed to make it better?

10 En la oficina

Tema 1 En la oficina

10-1 En la oficina. Write the names of the indicated objects in this office with the appropriate indefinite article (**un, una**).

1. _____
2. _____
3. _____

4. _____
5. _____
6. _____
7. _____
8. _____

10-2 ¿Cómo están? Which of the people pictured does the past participle of each verb describe?

la señora Ramos

Juan

Beti

MODELO   frustrar: **La señora Ramos está frustrada.**

1. desorganizar: _____

2. sentar: _____

3. relajar: _____

4. distraer (*to distract*): _____

5. enamorar: _____

6. enojar: _____

7. deprimir: _____

8. vestir de rebelde: _____

9. preocupar: _____

el padre

Marco

Luz

la madre

el hermanito

10-3 ¡Qué desorden! Describe the situation in Mario's room by filling in each blank with the correct form of the past participle of the logical verb from the box.

el cuarto de Mario

colgar (*to hang*)	desordenar	abrir
acostar	dejar	cerrar
sentar	pintar (*to paint*)	poner
apagar	hacer	

El cuarto de Mario está muy (1) _____. Un gato come pizza

(2) _____ en el escritorio y hay dos gatos más (3) _____

en la cama, que no está (4) _____. Hay un libro

(5) _____ sobre la alfombra y muchos otros libros

(6) _____ por todas partes. No hay ningún libro

(7) _____ en el estante, donde deben estar. No hay nadie

(8) _____ en la silla del escritorio y la computadora está

(9) _____. Hay dos pinturas (10) _____ en las paredes

y las paredes están (11) _____ de blanco.

10-4 Mi cuarto. Using the description of Mario's room in the preceding activity as an example, describe the current situation in your room, using at least six different past participles.

_____

_____

_____

_____

_____

_____

_____

_____

10-5 Entrevista. Complete the following questions with the past participles of the verbs in parentheses, as if a friend were talking to you. Then answer each question honestly.

1. Generalmente, ¿sólo te comunicas por Internet con personas _____ (conocer) o te comunicas también con desconocidos (*strangers*)?

   _____

2. ¿Recibes muchos correos electrónicos _____ (escribir) por desconocidos?

   ¿Siempre abres los correos electrónicos _____ (recibir) de desconocidos?

   _____

3. ¿Tienes un sitio web _____ (preferir)? ¿Cuál es? ¿Qué hay

   _____ (publicar) en ese sitio?

   _____

4. ¿Estás _____ (sorprender) a veces por las cosas

   _____ (decir) o _____ (ver) en Internet?

   _____

10-6 Diario. Describe your last day at work or at the university, using the past participle of at least six of the following verbs, or others: **ocupar, cansar, aburrir, preparar, preocupar** (*to worry*), **dormir, deprimir, enojar, emocionar** (*to excite*), **resfriar, equivocar.**

_____

_____

_____

_____

_____

_____

_____

_____

_____

¡A escuchar!

10-7 ¿Qué dice después? Stop the recording and complete the following
sentences with the correct forms of the past participles of the verbs given in
parentheses. Then turn on the recording and listen as one office worker makes
comments to another about the boss (**el jefe**), and read aloud the statement
from each pair that would logically come next. As you hear the correct statement
given, repeat it and write an **X** next to it.

1. _____ Todo está _____ (preparar) para la reunión (*meeting*) con los clientes.

   _____ Los informes (*reports*) para la reunión no están _____ (imprimir).

2. _____ Todos los clientes están _____ (sentar) y esperan _____
   (aburrir).

   _____ Todos los clientes están muy _____ (divertir) porque el jefe es muy
   cómico y les está contando chistes.

3. _____ El jefe se siente _____ (perder) si no tiene su presentación

   _____ (escribir) con *Power Point*.

   _____ Al jefe no le gustan las presentaciones _____ (hacer) con *Power Point*.

4. _____ La computadora está _____ (arreglar) y los informes están

   _____ (terminar *to finish*).

   _____ Los problemas con los informes y la computadora todavía no están _____
   (resolver).

10-8 El primer día. Listen as one friend talks to another about his first day at a new job. Then complete
the following sentences with the appropriate past participle used as an adjective, based on what you hear.

1. El amigo se ve muy _____. Él se siente un poco

   _____ y tiene los pulmones un poco _____.

2. Está _____ en el sofá porque tiene la espalda

   _____. Tuvo que mover unos muebles _____.

3. Ahora la oficina está _____ con la computadora

   _____ y la impresora _____. Todo está

   _____ para mañana, ¡menos él!

Tema 2 Un currículum vitae

10-9 Mi currículum. Using the **currículum vitae** on page 298 of the textbook as a model, complete the following one for yourself.

CURRÍCULUM VITAE

DATOS PERSONALES
Nombre y apellidos: _____
Fecha de nacimiento: _____
Lugar de nacimiento: _____
Estado civil: _____
Dirección: _____
Teléfono: _____
E-mail: _____

FORMACIÓN ACADÉMICA
Universitaria:
_____
_____

Preparatoria:
_____

Secundaria:
_____

Primaria:
_____
_____

EXPERIENCIA PROFESIONAL
_____
_____

IDIOMAS
_____
_____

INFORMÁTICA
_____
_____
_____
_____
_____

REFERENCIAS
_____

10-10 Búsqueda de trabajo. Complete the following conversation in which a person is looking for a new job, using words from the list that convey the same meaning as the words in parentheses.

aumento de sueldo	a tiempo parcial	la ubicación de
a nivel básico	además	un jefe
colegas	otros idiomas	de mal humor
a nivel alto	empleo	mudarme
a tiempo completo	gruñona	

— Dígame por qué quiere cambiar de trabajo.

— Primero, quiero trabajar (1) _____ (40 horas a la semana). Ahora sólo trabajo

(2) _____ (veinte horas a la semana). (3) _____

(También), hace dos años que tengo este (4) _____ (puesto) sin

(5) _____ (cambio de pago).

— ¿Hay otros motivos para esta decisión?

— El ambiente en la oficina es muy importante para mí. Es importante que tenga

(6) _____ (compañeros de trabajo) y (7) _____ (un

supervisor) simpáticos. Ahora tengo una supervisora (8) _____ (antipática).

Siempre está (9) _____ (enojada).

— ¿Habla Ud. (10) _____ (otras lenguas)?

— Sí, hablo inglés (11) _____ (muy bien) y francés

(12) _____ (un poco).

— ¿Le importa mucho (13) _____ (dónde está) la compañía?

— No, no me importa (14) _____ (cambiar de vecindario o ciudad).

10-11 ¿Hace cuánto tiempo? Imagine that a classmate from your Spanish class is talking about changes in different people's lives and activities. Use the preterite to say which activity they completed the indicated amount of time ago, and use the present tense to say what they have been doing since that time.

MODELO   Hace dos semanas que... (mi amigo: buscar trabajo, perder su trabajo)
              Hace dos semanas que mi amigo busca trabajo. /
              Hace dos semanas que perdió su trabajo.

1. Hace dos meses que... (mi novio: cambiar de trabajo / tener su nuevo trabajo)

_____

_____

2. Hace un año que... (mis vecinos: mudarse al lado / vivir aquí)

_____

_____

3. Hace medio año que... (mi hermana: tener un trabajo en diseño gráfico / graduarse de la universidad)

_____

_____

4. Hace un semestre que... (mi compañera de casa: sacar la licenciatura / hacer estudios graduados)

_____

_____

5. Hace dos años que... (yo: estudiar en esta universidad / terminar la preparatoria)

_____

_____

6. Hace unos minutos que... (nosotros: comenzar este ejercicio / hacerlo)

_____

_____

10-12 Diario. What are some changes that have taken place in your life over recent years? When did they occur? How long have things been as they are now? Write a paragraph describing a few such changes, using the preterite to tell how long ago the changes occurred and the present tense to say how long they have been as they are now. You may also use the imperfect tense to describe how things used to be before the change, compared to your present situation. Begin your paragraph with: **Mi vida (no) ha cambiado mucho recientemente...** (*My life has [not] changed much recently...*).

_____

_____

_____

_____

_____

_____

_____

_____

¡A escuchar!

10-13 Con una asesora de empleo. Listen to a conversation between an employment advisor and a recent college graduate. Then complete the following statements based on what you hear in the dialogue.

1. Hace tres meses que él _____.

2. Hace dos meses que _____.

3. En un trabajo, quiere sobre todo la oportunidad de ser creativo y _____.

4. La oportunidad de ser creativo tiene más importancia porque no quiere estar _____.

5. _____ es muy importante también porque

   quiere llevarse bien con sus _____.

6. _____ no es vital porque no le importa _____.

10-14 ¿Cuándo? It is Friday, December 17th at 11:15 a.m., and Yezenia is at the doctor's office rather than at work. Fill in the missing words from each statement and question that you hear. Then answer the question with a complete sentence.

1. Yezenia está enferma _____. ¿Qué día _____?

   _____

2. Yezenia _____ desde hace tres días. ¿Cuál _____ su

   último día en _____?

   _____

3. _____ Yezenia está en la sala de espera del

   doctor. ¿A qué hora _____?

   _____

10-15 Entrevista. Imagine that a classmate is asking you the following questions. Answer each one with a complete sentence in Spanish.

1. _____

2. _____

3. _____

4. _____

5. _____

Tema 3 ¿Qué experiencia tiene Ud.?

10-16 No, ¡te equivocas! A friend has everyone's profession confused. Clarify each person's profession by completing the sentences with the logical words.

MODELO

MODELO   No, mi tío no es **obrero** de la construcción sino (*but rather*) **obrero de fábrica.** Trabaja en la **fabricación** de autos.

1. Sí, mi hermana trabaja en ventas pero no es _____ de autos, sino

   _____ en un almacén.

2. Mi amiga Mónica no es recepcionista, sino _____. Pasa el día organizando la

   oficina y _____ los documentos en los archivadores.

3. Mi amiga Verónica es _____. Contesta el teléfono y recibe a los visitantes.

4. Mi padre no es contador sino _____ de _____
   humanos. Está encargado de organizar las entrevistas de empleo de la compañía.

5. Sí, tienes razón que mi hermano trabaja en transporte, pero no es _____ de
   taxi sino de autobús.

6. Yo no soy diseñadora gráfica sino _____. Yo mantengo la red (*network*) de
   computadoras de la compañía.

7. Mi esposo trabaja en el sistema educativo, pero no es profesor universitario. Es

   _____ en una _____ primaria.

10-17 Entrevistas. If an elementary school teacher and a computer programmer were being interviewed for jobs, which one would be asked if he/she has done each type of work listed? Write a logical question in the present perfect form for **Ud.** under the logical column. The first one has been done as an example.

diseñar muchas páginas web

trabajar mucho con niños

usar muchas bases de datos

dar clases en inglés y español

ver muchos libros para clases bilingües

programar una red de computadoras

hacer mucho teatro infantil

leer muchos cuentos indígenas para niños

tener muchos problemas de disciplina

enseñar en una escuela primaria

escribir programas en *UNIX*

resolver muchos problemas de virus

Un/a maestro/a de escuela primaria　　　**Un/a programador/a de computadoras**

_____　　　¿Ha diseñado muchas páginas web? _____

_____　　　_____

_____　　　_____

_____　　　_____

_____　　　_____

_____　　　_____

10-18 Tengo que despedirla. A boss is telling a colleague why he is firing his new secretary, who hasn't done anything right. Would he say that she has or has not done the following things? Complete the following sentences with the present prefect of the verbs in parentheses.

MODELO　　　**No ha terminado** (terminar) su trabajo.

1. _____ (dormir) en la oficina.

2. _____ (estar) de mal humor con frecuencia.

3. _____ (dejar) la oficina desordenada.

4. _____ (aprender) mucho sobre el trabajo.

5. _____ (llegar) tarde todos los días.

6. _____ (decir) cosas falsas.

7. _____ (romper) todos los muebles de la oficina.

8. _____ (hacer) mucho.

9. _____ (ser) una buena secretaria.

Nombre: _____ Fecha: _____

10-19 Un colega mentiroso. Imagine that you have a colleague who takes sole credit for everything that goes right in the office, but he says that everyone is responsible for the things that go wrong. Write sentences in the appropriate column in the present perfect. The first item in each column has already been done as an example.

tener problemas con unos clientes   pagar demasiado por la publicidad
resolver los problemas con los clientes   escribir cosas equivocadas en la publicidad
diseñar la nueva página web   perder unos clientes
decir siempre la verdad   hacer la mayor parte *(most)* del trabajo

Yo...	**Nosotros...**
He resuelto los problemas con los clientes.	Hemos tenido problemas con unos clientes.
_____	_____
_____	_____
_____	_____
_____	_____

10-20 Diario. Imagine that someone famous is looking for work and is being interviewed by a job counselor at an unemployment office. Write a conversation in which the counselor first asks the person's name, then asks about what experience he/she has, using a variety of verbs in the present perfect. You may also talk about how long he/she has been doing something that he/she still does, using the present tense, or how long ago or for how long he/she did something in the past, using the preterite. Pick any celebrity you wish and use your imagination to create an interesting conversation.

_____

_____

_____

_____

_____

_____

_____

¡A escuchar!

10-21 El día de Olga. Here are all the things that Olga has already done by 8:15 this morning. Answer each question you hear by saying that she has already done the activity if it is shown, or that she has not done it yet if it is not pictured. If it is something that she has already done, indicate the number of the question under the corresponding illustration. One illustration will have two numbers. When you hear the correct answer, repeat it.

MODELO 1   You hear: ¿Ya ha hablado por teléfono con su novio?
                  You answer: **No, todavía no ha hablado por teléfono con su novio.**
                  You hear: No, todavía no ha hablado por teléfono con su novio.
                  You repeat: **No, todavía no ha hablado por teléfono con su novio.**

MODELO 2   You hear: ¿Ya ha hecho los cheques para pagar las cuentas?
                  You answer: **Sí, ya ha hecho los cheques para pagar las cuentas.**
                  You hear: Sí, ya ha hecho los cheques para pagar las cuentas.
                  You repeat: **Sí, ya ha hecho los cheques para pagar las cuentas.**
                  You write: *The number of the question under the corresponding illustration.*

Modelo 2

10-22 Entrevista. Imagine that a classmate is asking you the following questions. Answer each one with a complete sentence in Spanish.

1. _____

2. _____

3. _____

4. _____

5. _____

Tema 4 ¿Qué han hecho?

10-23 ¿Quién lo ha hecho? Which employee from the list has done the following things today? Write sentences replacing the italicized direct objects with pronouns.

> el programador   la contadora   el recepcionista   el diseñador gráfico
> el secretario   la directora de recursos humanos   la supervisora

MODELO archivar *todos los documentos*
El secretario los ha archivado.

1. recibir *muchas solicitudes de empleo*

_____

2. evaluar *los progresos de los nuevos empleados*

_____

3. arreglar *los programas de computadora que han fallado*

_____

4. recibir *a todos los visitantes*

_____

5. hacer *los diseños para la nueva publicidad*

_____

6. pagar *los impuestos*

_____

10-24 ¿Quién se lo ha hecho a quién? Which person listed in parentheses has logically completed the indicated task for or to the other person or thing? Write sentences with indirect object pronouns, as in the **modelo.**

MODELO ofrecer café (los visitantes / la recepcionista)
La recepcionista les ha ofrecido café a los visitantes.

1. presentar una solicitud de empleo (pocos candidatos / la oficina de recursos humanos)

_____

2. traer los documentos para la reunión (la supervisora / el secretario)

_____

3. dar su evaluación (la supervisora / los empleados)

_____

4. pedir ayuda con su computadora (la contadora / el programador)

_____

5. distribuir el correo (el secretario / todos los empleados)

_____

6. ofrecer empleo (una de las candidatas / el director de recursos humanos)

_____

7. decir su decisión (los empleados / la supervisora)

_____

8. devolver los documentos para archivarlos (la supervisora / el secretario)

_____

9. hacer los cambios (el programador / la página web)

_____

Now reword the answers you gave above, replacing the direct objects with pronouns.

MODELO   **La recepcionista se lo ha ofrecido a los visitantes.**

1. _____

2. _____

3. _____

4. _____

5. _____

6. _____

7. _____

8. _____

9. _____

10-25 ¿Qué ha realizado ya? Imagine that an academic or employment advisor is asking you the following questions. Answer each one using a direct object, indirect object, or reflexive pronoun.

MODELO   ¿Ya ha tomado todos los cursos optativos (*electives*)?
            Sí, ya los he tomado todos. / No, no los he tomado todos.

1. ¿Ya se ha graduado de la preparatoria?

   _____

2. ¿Ya ha obtenido la licenciatura?

   _____

3. ¿Ya ha terminado (*finished*) su primer año de estudios universitarios?

   _____

4. ¿Ha utilizado alguna vez la hoja de cálculo *Excel*?

   _____

5. ¿Cuántas veces se ha mudado durante los últimos cinco años?

   _____

6. ¿Ha preparado su currículum vitae recientemente?

   _____

10-26 Diario. Make a list of several goals you wanted to accomplish over the last few years of your studies, your career, or in life in general. Then explain what you have been able to do, and what you have not been able to do yet.

_____

_____

_____

_____

_____

_____

_____

_____

¡A escuchar!

10-27 ¿Quién lo ha hecho? Answer the questions you hear with the name of the logical employee from those listed, using direct object pronouns to say that they still haven't done what they need to do. Then repeat as you hear the correct answer, and write the missing part of the sentence next to the appropriate employee.

MODELO   You hear: ¿Ha terminado la nueva página web?
                     You say: **No, el programador todavía no la ha terminado.**
                     You hear: No, el programador todavía no la ha terminado.
                     You repeat: **No, el programador todavía no la ha terminado.**
                     You write: *The end of the sentence next to the name of the employee mentioned.*

a. No, la supervisora todavía no _____.

b. No, el programador todavía no **la ha terminado** _____.

c. No, el secretario todavía no _____.

d. No, el director de recursos humanos todavía no _____.

e. No, la recepcionista todavía no _____.

f. No, la contadora todavía no _____.

g. No, el diseñador gráfico todavía no _____.

10-28 Todavía no. Using direct object pronouns with the verbs listed under the illustrations of the employees being described, say that they have not finished their task, as in the **modelo**. Then repeat as you hear the correct answer, and indicate the number of the question under the corresponding illustration.

MODELO   You hear: El contador ha calculado los impuestos.
                     You see: *The verb **pagar** under the illustration of the accountant.*
                     You say: **El contador ha calculado los impuestos pero todavía no los ha pagado.**
                     You hear: El contador ha calculado los impuestos pero todavía no los ha pagado.
                     You repeat: **El contador ha calculado los impuestos pero todavía no los ha pagado.**
                     You write: *The number of the question under the illustration of the accountant.*

publicar en Internet   entrenar   pagar   traer a mi oficina

_____   _____   **Modelo**   _____

Tema 5 En el banco

10-29 Trámites bancarios. Complete the following sentences with logical nouns from the same word family as the italicized verb.

1. El Sr. Santana quiere obtener un _____. El Sr. Elizondo es banquero y le va a *prestar* diez mil dólares.

2. El Sr. Elizondo le da _____ al Sr. Santana porque *cree* que va a devolver el dinero con interés.

3. El Sr. Santana tendrá que hacer un _____ cada mes. Va a *pagar* una tasa de interés del siete por ciento.

4. La Sra. Molina hace un _____ de un cajero automático. Quiere *retirar* cien dólares.

5. El banco *debe* pagar lo que los clientes *deben* si utilizan su tarjeta de _____.

6. La Srta. Benítez tiene que *depositar* su cheque en persona porque no tiene _____ directo.

7. La Srta. Benítez trata de *contar* con cuidado cuánto retira de su _____ corriente.

8. La Srta. Benítez siempre deposita la cuarta parte de su sueldo en su cuenta de

_____. Le gusta *ahorrar* dinero.

9. No me gusta *cargar* mucho en mi tarjeta de crédito porque pago interés y otros

_____.

10-30 Reacciones. Imagine that the following things happen to you. Say whether you are happy about them or bothered by them.

Me molesta que... Me alegro de que...

MODELO   Hay muchos cargos en su tarjeta de crédito por cosas que Ud. no compró.
Me molesta que haya muchos cargos en mi tarjeta de crédito por cosas que no compré.

1. La policía ha arrestado a la persona que estaba utilizando el número de su tarjeta de crédito.

_____

2. La persona que utilizó su tarjeta de crédito ha devuelto todas las cosas que compró.

_____

3. El banco le ha cobrado interés sobre los cargos de esa persona.

_____

4. El banco ha perdido su cheque de depósito directo.

_____

5. Su banco ha abierto una sucursal a cinco minutos de su casa.

_____

6. La nueva sucursal cerca de su casa no tiene cajero automático.

_____

7. La nueva sucursal está abierta hasta las siete de la tarde todos los días.

_____

10-31 Consejos de una amiga. A friend is giving you information about a job opening that interests you where she works. Complete the following statements logically by putting one verb in the present subjunctive and the other in the present perfect subjunctive, according to the context. Use the **tú** form unless otherwise indicated.

MODELO   Estoy contenta de que ya **te hayas graduado** (graduarse) de la universidad.
            Es necesario que los candidatos **tengan** (tener) la licenciatura.

1. Quieren que el nuevo empleado _____ (conocer) otras culturas.

   Van a estar contentos de que _____ (vivir) en varios países.

2. También les va a gustar que _____ (saber) otro idioma.

   Es preferible que los candidatos _____ (estudiar) una lengua extranjera.

3. Es necesario que _____ (tener) experiencia con una compañía como ésta.

   Es mejor que ya _____ (hacer) este tipo de trabajo.

4. Es bueno que ya _____ (presentar) tu solicitud.

   Es preferible que la oficina de recursos humanos _____ (recibir) las solicitudes temprano.

5. Es una lástima que _____ (cambiar) tanto de empleo.

   No quieren que los empleados _____ (irse) después de ser entrenados.

6. Me alegro de que el director de recursos humanos _____ (decidir) entrevistarte para el puesto.

   Es importante que _____ (llegar) a tiempo para la entrevista.

10-32 Diario. Think of a friend or family member who has had some problems recently at work, at school, or in a relationship. Write a paragraph to him/her in which you express your sentiments about what has happened, then give recommendations of what to do to resolve the problems.

_____

_____

_____

_____

_____

_____

_____

¡A escuchar!

10-33 Un préstamo. Listen as a couple discusses a bank transaction and complete their conversation with the missing words.

— Temo que _____ para comprar el coche nuevo.

— ¿Por qué dudas que _____ el dinero? Siempre _____

todas nuestras cuentas a tiempo y tenemos _____.

— No sé. Es mucho dinero. Nunca _____ un banco.

— Me sorprende que _____.

_____, ¿verdad?

— Sí, voy a presentarlos en el banco esta mañana.

— Tenemos que hacerlo pronto. Me molesta que _____

esta semana, y _____ pronto.

10-34 Sentimientos. Imagine that a friend makes the statements you hear. React to each statement using one of the expressions of emotion listed. Then repeat the correct answer as you hear it again and place an **X** next to the expression of emotion that is used.

MODELO   You see: _____ Me alegro de que... _____ Es una lástima que...
                You hear: He perdido mi trabajo.
                You say: **Es una lástima que hayas perdido tu trabajo.**
                You hear: Es una lástima que hayas perdido tu trabajo.
                You repeat: **Es una lástima que hayas perdido tu trabajo.**
                You indicate: _____ Me alegro de que... __**X**__ Es una lástima que...

1. _____ Me alegro de que...   _____ Me molesta que...

2. _____ Estoy contento/a de que...   _____ Estoy triste de que...

3. _____ Me alegro de que...   _____ Tengo miedo de que...

4. _____ Me encanta que...   _____ Me sorprende que...

5. _____ Es bueno que...   _____ Es malo que...

6. _____ Estoy contento/a de que...   _____ Me molesta que...

7. _____ Estoy contento/a de que...   _____ Temo que...

8. _____ Es bueno que...   _____ Siento que...

¡Trato hecho!

10-35 En la red. Search the Web for job offers in Spanish-speaking areas, such as those offered on Web sites like http://www.Monster.es. You may find other similar Web sites by searching for *ofertas de empleo* or *bolsa de empleos*. Write the address of the site you consult below and give the requested information that follows, writing your answers in Spanish.

www._____

1. What are the category headings of areas of work for which job offers are listed?

   _____

   _____

   _____

   _____

   _____

   _____

   _____

2. Which is the area of work that interests you the most?

   _____

3. Write down or print out and attach two job offers for which you think you are a good candidate.

   _____

   _____

   _____

   _____

   _____

   _____

   _____

10-36 Composición. Write the text of an e-mail explaining why one of the job offers you found in the preceding activities for **En la red** is a good job for you. In the first paragraph, explain what interests you about the position and talk about how your character and skills make you a good candidate for this job. In the second paragraph, tell whether you have related experience from previous work, and talk about the related studies you have done. In the final paragraph, ask any questions you have about the position, such as benefits, location, etc.

_____

_____

_____

_____

_____

_____

_____

_____

_____

_____

_____

_____

_____

_____

_____

_____

_____

_____

_____

11   En las noticias

Tema 1 ¿Cómo se informa Ud.?

11-1 Para todos los gustos. Gonzalo is telling us about the different television programs and types of media that his family likes. Complete his description with the appropriate word from the list.

pronóstico del tiempo	salas de chat	programas de entrevistas	documentales
noticiero	prensa invitados	economía noticias	televisión

- A mi padre le gusta mucho ver el (1) _____ de las nueve de la noche. Le

  interesan especialmente las (2) _____ de Latinoamérica.

- A mi hermana le encantan los (3) _____,

  especialmente cuando hay (4) _____ famosos.

- Yo no veo mucho la (5) _____, pero me interesan especialmente los

  (6) _____ porque están basados en historias reales.

- Mi abuelo lee la (7) _____ todos los días; le interesa saber cómo está la

  (8) _____ del país. Y en la televisión siempre mira el

  (9) _____ para saber si va a llover.

- Mis hermanos pasan mucho tiempo en Internet, especialmente en las

  (10) _____, donde pueden hablar con sus amigos de todo el mundo.

11-2 Definiciones. Using the vocabulary that you learned in this **Tema,** determine the appropriate word for each definition.

1. _____ es un programa que informa de la actualidad del país y de los países
   internacionales.

2. _____ son programas que cuentan una historia real o examinan un problema
   social o político.

3. _____ es una herramienta (*tool*) para encontrar información en Internet.

4. _____ son programas donde el/la anfitrión/anfitriona les hace preguntas a
   los invitados.

5. _____ son lugares en la red donde las personas charlan (*chat*) sobre temas o
   intereses personales.

11-3 Conexiones. Rafael is telling us about his friend Guzmán's experience in the news world as a journalist at **Univisión**. Combine the following sentences with the relative pronoun **que** to describe Guzmán's career and background.

1. Tengo un amigo del colegio. Mi amigo del colegio se llama Guzmán y es presentador de noticias en una cadena de televisión.

   _____

2. Es una cadena de televisión en español en Estados Unidos. Esta cadena tiene una audiencia hispana muy grande.

   _____

3. Guzmán estudió la carrera de periodismo. La carrera de periodismo le dio la oportunidad de entrar en el mundo de la televisión.

   _____

4. Primero, Guzmán estuvo trabajando en la cadena de televisión mexicana Azteca México. La cadena de televisión Azteca México es una de las más importantes del país.

   _____

5. Guzmán hizo un trabajo excelente en la televisión mexicana. Este trabajo le abrió las puertas a la televisión hispana de Estados Unidos.

   _____

6. Guzmán tiene un trabajo de mucha responsabilidad. Este trabajo le permite conocer a personas muy interesantes del mundo de la economía y la política.

   _____

11-4 ¡Cuántos pronombres! Complete the following questions with the relative pronouns **que, quien(es),** or **lo que,** as appropriate. Then answer each question.

1. ¿Te informas de _____ pasa en el mundo? ¿Cuáles son las noticias

   _____ te interesan más?

   _____

   _____

2. ¿Cuáles son los invitados de los programas de entrevistas en _____ la audiencia está más interesada? ¿Estás interesado/a en _____ dicen esas personas?

_____

_____

3. Cuando lees la prensa, ¿quieres saber _____ está ocurriendo en los países de Latinoamérica o sólo lees las noticias _____ hablan de Estados Unidos?

_____

_____

4. ¿Cuáles son los programas de televisión _____ prefieren los estudiantes en tu universidad? ¿Te identificas con esos programas _____ son populares entre los estudiantes?

_____

_____

5. ¿Cuál es el buscador _____ más usan los estudiantes en tu universidad? ¿Controla tu universidad _____ pueden ver los estudiantes en Internet en las computadoras del campus?

_____

_____

11-5 Diario How do you and most students you know stay informed (**informarse**)? How did your parents and grandparents used to stay informed when they were your age? Write a paragraph explaining how the news media have changed.

_____

_____

_____

_____

_____

_____

¡A escuchar!

11-6 ¿Qué ven? ¿Qué creen? Listen to the following interviews with people about the type of television programs that they watch and their reaction towards them. Complete the exchanges with the words that you hear.

A. — Buenas tardes, estamos haciendo una encuesta sobre los hábitos de televisión de las amas de casa.

¿Puede decirme cuáles son los programas (1) _____?

— Sí, claro, me gustan los programas con invitados (2) _____.

— Ah, le gustan los (3) _____.

B.— Hola, estamos haciendo una encuesta sobre los programas (4) _____.

¿Te interesa (5) _____?

— No, no mucho. Prefiero ir al cine. Me gustan mucho las películas sobre la naturaleza

(6) _____ de todas partes del mundo.

— Sí, entonces ves especialmente (7) _____.

C. — Buenas tardes, estamos haciendo una encuesta sobre los hábitos de televisión de los jubilados.

¿Hablo con alguien a (8) _____?

— Sí, pero no me gusta (9) _____, por eso sólo veo los programas

(10) _____.

— Muy bien, por la noche le gusta mirar los (11) _____.

11-7 El show de Cristina. Complete the following information about a popular show among Hispanics, *El show de Cristina,* broadcast by **Univisión**. Fill in the blanks with the words that you hear.

(1) _____ de la televisión hispana (2) _____ tiene

gran popularidad en Estados Unidos es Cristina Saralegui. Ella es (3) _____

excelente en su programa *El show de Cristina*, y recibe a invitados (4) _____

son muy populares en el mundo de la farándula (*entertainment*). (5) _____

_____ de Cristina emite en español, (6) _____

gusta mucho a la audiencia hispana de Estados Unidos. Con su programa, Cristina realiza

(7) _____ importante a la televisión (8) _____

se ve en este país.

Tema 2 ¿Qué noticias locales y nacionales hay?

11-8 ¡Qué mundo! Complete the following comments about social problems that affect today's society using the relative pronouns **que** and **quien(es)**, and the vocabulary that you learned in this **Tema**.

1. Desafortunadamente, son muchas las amas de casa _____ reciben abusos de sus esposos. Son

   víctimas de la _____.

2. Hay muchas personas _____ vienen de otros países para trabajar a Estados Unidos. La

   _____ desde Latinoamérica es especialmente importante y hay muchos

   _____ ilegales en el país para _____ no hay seguro médico u otros

   beneficios.

3. Muchos jóvenes de hoy _____ viven en barrios marginados (*on the edge of society*), acaban (*end up*)

   en grupos de violencia organizada. Se hacen miembros de las _____.

4. Hay familias para _____ es importante recibir _____

   porque sus sueldos no son suficientes para mantener a todos sus miembros.

5. En algunas partes del país las personas han perdido sus trabajos y la tasa de

   _____ es muy alta. Nuestra economía debe atender a las necesidades de estas

   regiones _____ necesitan el establecimiento de nuevos negocios.

11-9 El mundo de la política. Read the report that journalist Rita Ramos gives from Washington regarding the latest elections in the United States. Complete the information with the appropriate words from the list.

educación	Congreso	presidente	candidatos	leyes
desempleo	jueces	elecciones	sociedad	

Los ciudadanos americanos han elegido recientemente a su nuevo (1) _____.

Este año las (2) _____ han sido muy interesantes. Los dos

(3) _____ realizaron grandes esfuerzos durante sus campañas y hablaron sobre

temas que preocupan (*worry*) a la (4) _____, como la

(5) _____ y el (6) _____. Vamos a ver cuáles son las

(7) _____ que el gobierno va a pasar al (8) _____ y

cuál va a ser la reacción de los (9) _____ a estas propuestas de ley.

11-10 La voz de la universidad. Complete the following comments about social and political issues that concern university students with the indicative or subjunctive, as appropriate.

1. Los estudiantes buscamos representantes políticos que _____ (ser) honestos y

   que _____ (comprender) los problemas de la universidad.

2. Queremos líderes que _____ (preocuparse) por las cuestiones de educación y

   que _____ (mirar) hacia el futuro de los jóvenes.

3. Los estudiantes tenemos preocupaciones que _____ (afectar) a nuestro futuro

   y que _____ (necesitar) ser oídas.

4. No hay ningún candidato en la actualidad que _____ (entender) nuestras

   preocupaciones ni que _____ (responder) a nuestras peticiones.

5. Nuestros representantes universitarios son estudiantes que _____ (conocer)

   muy bien las leyes y que _____ (luchar) por los derechos de su gente.

6. Se necesitan más representantes en la política que _____ (pensar) en las

   prioridades de los universitarios y _____ (querer) ayudarlos.

11-11 ¿Conocen a alguien que...? Read the following answers to questions you might ask a friend and write out a logical question that would elicit each one.

MODELO   — **¿Conoces a alguien que busque trabajo?**
              — Sí, conozco a muchas personas que buscan trabajo.

1. —_____

   — Sí, conozco a un candidato que habla español.

2. —_____

   — Sí, conocemos a varios chicos que son miembros de la pandilla de nuestro barrio.

3. —_____

   — Sí, hay muchas personas en mi ciudad que no tienen trabajo.

4. —_____

   — Sí, conocemos a muchos votantes que están descontentos con los resultados de las elecciones.

5. —_____

   — Sí, hay muchos estudiantes a quienes les preocupa la seguridad nacional.

11-12 En su universidad. Answer the following questions according to your personal experience at the university and in discussions with your friends.

1. ¿Hay mucho interés político entre los estudiantes de su universidad? ¿Qué grupos políticos hay en su universidad?

_____

_____

2. ¿Qué función tienen los representantes del Senado de su universidad? ¿Conoce a algún representante?

_____

_____

_____

3. ¿Es buena la situación económica de su universidad? ¿En qué gasta el dinero su universidad?

_____

_____

_____

11-13 Diario. Are you satisfied with the current national political scene? List some of the social aspects that concern you and your family. Then describe the characteristics that in your opinion a good politician should have. List the different priorities that he/she should establish during his/her term.

_____

_____

_____

_____

_____

_____

_____

_____

¡A escuchar!

11-14 ¿Qué se necesita? Listen to the following interviews asking citizens about different issues, and fill in the blanks with what you hear.

1. — ¿Cree que se necesitan leyes que _____ más a los ciudadanos?

   — Sí, el gobierno debe dedicar más dinero a la _____.

2. — ¿Cree que se necesitan leyes que _____ los impuestos?

   — Sí, este país necesita una _____ de su economía.

3. — ¿Cree que se necesitan leyes que _____ la situación de los trabajadores?

   — Sí, porque hoy en día hay mucho _____ en el país.

4. — ¿Cree que se necesitan leyes que _____ a las necesidades de las escuelas?

   — Sí, la educación debe ser una _____ del gobierno.

5. — ¿Cree que se necesitan iniciativas que _____ la participación de las mujeres en la política?

   — Sí, creo que una mujer candidata a _____ atraería (*would attract*) a muchas votantes.

11-15 Hablando de política. Esperanza and Eduardo have different positions on social and political issues. Listen to their conversation and fill in the missing words below.

— No estoy de acuerdo contigo, Eduardo. La (1) _____ es un problema serio en los campus universitarios. Parece que vives en otro mundo.

— Esperanza, no seas exagerada. En la universidad no hay (2) _____ que

   (3) _____ problemas ni situaciones que (4) _____

   peligrosas (*dangerous*) para los estudiantes.

— Mira, Eduardo, ¿tú no escuchas las (5) _____? Cada día

   (6) _____ la seguridad en los campus. Más y más estudiantes son víctimas de

   (7) _____ y en una (8) _____ publicada en el

   periódico de la universidad, los estudiantes dicen que tienen miedo a salir del campus por la noche.

— Bueno, Esperanza, la seguridad en el campus no es un (9) _____ que me

   (10) _____, así que vamos a dejarlo, ¿vale?

Nombre: _____   Fecha: _____

Tema 3 ¿Qué noticias internacionales hay?

11-16 ¿Cuál es el problema? Complete the following definitions with the noun that fits from the vocabulary that you learned in this **Tema**.

1. _____ es una enfermedad que afecta especialmente a los niños pobres.

2. _____ son grupos organizados que amenazan la seguridad nacional.

3. _____ es una concentración de personas que protestan contra una decisión del gobierno.

4. _____ es un movimiento de la tierra que puede causar mucha destrucción en las ciudades.

5. _____ son las muestras de los cambios positivos o negativos de la economía.

6. _____ es un problema que afecta a muchas regiones de Latinoamérica que no tienen suficientes recursos económicos.

11-17 ¡Cuántos interrogantes! Cristina is very concerned about the problems that affect today's world, and she wonders when the situation will improve. Complete each of her questions about the future with the future tense of the verb in parentheses and the appropriate word from the list.

recursos naturales	ayuda humanitaria	inundaciones	protestas	terrorismo	pobreza

1. ¿Cuándo _____ (llegar) la _____ a las regiones afectadas por el huracán?

2. ¿_____ (continuar) las _____ contra la guerra?

3. ¿Cuándo se _____ (imponer) medidas para combatir el

   _____?

4. ¿Cuándo _____ (revisar) el gobierno las leyes de utilización de los

   _____?

5. ¿Cuándo se _____ (producir) una mejora de la situación de la

   _____ de algunos países de África?

6. ¿_____ (haber) más terremotos e _____ en Centroamérica?

11-18 No, no creo. Ricardo has a very pessimistic attitude toward world problems. For each of his statements, form a logical question with the future tense.

MODELO — **¿Mejorará el problema de la pobreza mundial pronto?**

— No, no creo que el problema de la pobreza mundial mejore pronto.

1. — _____

— Sí, es probable que haya más protestas contra la guerra.

2. — _____

— Sí, es posible que Estados Unidos invada otro país.

3. — _____

— No, no creo que mejore el problema de la malnutrición en los países pobres.

4. — _____

— No, no creo que el gobierno imponga sanciones contra la devastación de la costa.

5. — _____

— No, no creo que el gobierno recorte los impuestos en los próximos meses.

11-19 ¿Qué pasará si...? What will happen if the government or individuals do not take responsibility for the future of our world? Form sentences using the present tense in the clause with **si** (*if*) and the future in the result clause. Note that the *if*-clause is not always the first one.

MODELO los países construir canales / reducirse el riesgo (*risk*) de inundaciones
Si los países construyen canales, se reducirá el riesgo de inundaciones.

1. utilizarse todos los recursos naturales / la Tierra morir

_____

2. nunca vivir en paz (nosotros) / no parar (*stop*) el terrorismo

_____

3. haber más catástrofes naturales / continuar el calentamiento global

_____

4. las Naciones Unidas no llegar a un acuerdo / empeorar las relaciones internacionales

_____

5. los votantes protestar contra las acciones del gobierno / el gobierno no revisar las leyes

_____

6. el mundo ver una mejora del medioambiente (*environment*) / los gobiernos imponer sanciones contra las empresas que contaminen

_____

11-20 Preguntas para el presidente. Think of four questions that you would like to ask the president of the United States. Use the future tense and the vocabulary that you have learned so far in the chapter.

1. _____

2. _____

3. _____

4. _____

11-21 Diario. Are you informed about what happens in the world? How do you get international news? What are the problems that concern you the most? Do you think that the current problems that affect the world will be solved? What can the government and the citizens do to improve these situations? Write a paragraph in response to these questions using the vocabulary that you learned in this **Tema**, the future tense, and the subjunctive, when necessary.

_____

_____

_____

_____

_____

_____

_____

_____

¡A escuchar!

11-22 Noticias internacionales. Listen to the information that Santos Lafuente reports on *Noticiero de las dos* and complete his report with the words that you hear.

Muy buenas tardes. Esta tarde en (1) _____, tenemos las siguientes noticias. Hoy

en la capital, miles de personas (2) _____ contra la guerra y

(3) _____ al presidente con no apoyar su candidatura a las elecciones si los

(4) _____ continúan.

Las Naciones Unidas se (5) _____ el próximo mes para

(6) _____ las amenazas de (7) _____ internacional y

discutir nuevos (8) _____.

El gobierno (9) _____ un aumento de impuestos, que

(10) _____ una respuesta negativa de parte de las empresas.

Los nuevos (11) _____ muestran una (12) _____ en

la tasa de desempleo anual.

Los altos índices de contaminación y el aumento de los automóviles en las ciudades

(13) _____ el problema ya grave del (14) _____. Y a

continuación la actualidad del deporte con Pablo Salgado.

11-23 Predicciones. Answer the questions that you hear, filling in the missing information and putting the verbs in the future tense. You will then hear the correct answer. Repeat it and write the missing words.

Modelo	You see:	El candidato de California _____.
	You hear:	¿Quién cree que gane las próximas elecciones?
	You say:	**El candidato de California ganará las próximas elecciones.**
	You hear:	El candidato de California ganará las próximas elecciones.
	You write:	El candidato de California **ganará las próximas elecciones**.

1. Los países del Oriente Medio (*Middle East*) _____.

2. Las víctimas de la catástrofe _____.

3. Los representantes del Congreso _____.

4. El terrorismo _____.

5. La economía y la seguridad nacional _____.

6. Los sectores de tecnología y comunicaciones _____.

7. La contaminación y la salud pública _____.

8. _____ en Florida.

Tema 4 ¿Qué cambiará y cuándo?

11-24 ¿Será mejor el futuro? Complete the following predictions about a better future with the future form of the verb in parentheses and the appropriate word from the list.

oportunidades	garantizados	diversidad	problemas ecológicos	estabilidad económica

1. En el futuro, los servicios de salud _____ (estar)

   _____ para todos los ciudadanos y _____ (haber)

   más tratamientos para las enfermedades.

2. En los próximos años, los países _____ (asegurar) una mayor cooperación

   internacional y _____ (aumentar) la _____.

3. El futuro de la educación es muy bueno. Las instituciones _____

   (beneficiarse) de los avances en tecnología y _____ (haber) más

   _____ para todos los estudiantes.

4. En las grandes ciudades se _____ (reducir) la contaminación y no

   _____ (existir) tantos _____.

5. En el futuro, las empresas _____ (imponer) leyes para la aceptación de

   trabajadores de distintas etnias y se _____ (ver) más

   _____ en los lugares de trabajo.

11-25 Imaginen. How are our lifestyles going to be in fifty years? Answer the following questions with the logical response from the list.

manejar coches eléctricos
haber menos conflictos y más cooperación internacional
vivir más tiempo con los avances en medicina
tener aviones privados en vez de coches
hablar por Internet y no usar el teléfono celular
trabajar desde casa con los avances en tecnología
haber estabilidad y los índices de desempleo ser más bajos

MODELO ¿Cómo será nuestra salud? **Viviremos más tiempo con los avances en medicina.**

1. ¿Cómo serán los automóviles? _____

2. ¿Cómo serán las oficinas? _____

3. ¿Cómo será la seguridad nacional? _____

4. ¿Cómo serán las comunicaciones? _____

5. ¿Cómo serán los viajes? _____

6. ¿Cómo será la economía? _____

11-26 ¿Qué pasará cuando...? Link the statements in the left column with the logical endings from the right column. Then form sentences with the potential event in the subjunctive (left column) and the verb of the main clause in the future (right column). The first one has been done as an example.

Hasta que las personas no <u>aceptar</u> la diversidad,...	<u>haber</u> guerras.
	<u>haber</u> muchos cambios.
Mientras los gobiernos no <u>colaborar</u>,...	<u>haber</u> curas para las enfermedades.
Cuando <u>haber</u> elecciones,...	<u>haber</u> racismo en la sociedad.
Mientras <u>continuar</u> los avances en medicina,...	<u>haber</u> verdadera cooperación internacional.
Hasta que no <u>mejorar</u> la educación,...	no <u>haber</u> oportunidades iguales para los
Cuando los países <u>llegar</u> a un acuerdo, (*agreement*)...	jóvenes.

MODELO   Hasta que las personas no acepten la diversidad, habrá racismo en la sociedad.

1. _____.

2. _____.

3. _____.

4. _____.

5. _____.

11-27 Circunstancias. Esteban seems to have his future all figured out. Read the circumstances that will make him accomplish the following things, and complete the sentences with the verbs in parentheses in the future or subjunctive form for **él**.

1. No _____ (casarse) hasta que no _____ (tener) un

   buen trabajo y estabilidad económica.

2. No _____ (comprar) una casa hasta que no _____
   (saber) dónde quiere vivir para siempre.

3. _____ (quedarse) en el mismo trabajo hasta que _____

   (conocer) otras oportunidades.

4. _____ (estudiar) en la universidad hasta que _____

   (terminar) su maestría.

5. _____ (vivir) con sus padres hasta que _____
(ahorrar) suficiente dinero para vivir solo.

6. No _____ (viajar) mucho hasta que no _____
(pagar) sus deudas (*debts*) de la universidad.

7. No _____ (estar) satisfecho hasta que no _____
(hacer) realidad sus sueños.

Now make these sentences true for you with your ideas and plans for the future.

1. _____

2. _____

3. _____

4. _____

5. _____

6. _____

7. _____

11-28 Diario. How do you think our current values will change in a more globalized world? What are some of the advantages and disadvantages of a more globalized economy? Do you think that all countries will benefit equally from globalization? Write a paragraph responding to these questions and explain your position for or against more globalization and the changes it will bring.

_____

_____

_____

_____

_____

_____

_____

_____

¡A escuchar!

11-29 La globalización. Listen to the following arguments in favor of and against globalization, repeat each one, and fill in the missing words. Then indicate whether each argument is in favor of or against globalization by marking **a favor** or **en contra** with an **X**.

MODELO   You see: _____ un sentido (*a sense*) _____

               You hear: Habrá un sentido de comunidad internacional.

               You repeat: **Habrá un sentido de comunidad internacional.**

               You write: <u>**Habrá**</u> un sentido <u>**de comunidad internacional**</u>.

               You indicate: <u>**X**</u> a favor _____ en contra

1. _____ con la globalización. _____ a favor _____ en contra

2. _____ para las enfermedades. _____ a favor _____ en contra

3. _____ las comunicaciones. _____ a favor _____ en contra

4. _____ más impersonales. _____ a favor _____ en contra

5. _____ entre países. _____ a favor _____ en contra

6. _____ a los pobres. _____ a favor _____ en contra

7. _____ la pobreza. _____ a favor _____ en contra

8. _____ internacionales. _____ a favor _____ en contra

9. _____ entre las sociedades. _____ a favor _____ en contra

10. _____ parte de su identidad. _____ a favor _____ en contra

11-30 ¿Y tú? Imagine that a classmate asks you the following questions about your future. Answer each question with a complete sentence.

1. _____

2. _____

3. _____

4. _____

5. _____

Tema 5 ¿Será posible?

11-31 La fascinación por la farándula. Ángeles is challenging Marga's fascination with celebrities. Complete their conversation with the appropriate words from the list.

| telenovelas | acusados | chismes | farándula | rupturas | rumor |

— No entiendo cómo te puede interesar tanto el mundo de la (1) _____, Marga.

— Bueno, me gusta saber cuáles son los últimos (2) _____ de los famosos. No hay nada malo en ello, ¿no crees?

— No, pero, ¿por qué son tan fascinantes las (3) _____ y las reconciliaciones de los famosos?

— Son fascinantes porque te dan una visión real de los protagonistas de las (4)

_____, que siempre tienen problemas ficticios.

— Sí, pero los famosos no son personas importantes que curen enfermedades o lleguen a acuerdos

internacionales de paz. Muchas veces son (5) _____ de abuso de drogas y son

arrestados, creando escándalos muy grandes y dando mal ejemplo.

— En eso tienes razón, pero muchas veces esas noticias son sólo un (6) _____ y no hay nada cierto en las acusaciones.

11-32 ¡Cuántos chismes! Write the logical question one might make wondering about the following situations. Change the italicized verbs of the items from the list to the future tense.

¿*Tienen* un romance?   ¿Qué *ha* hecho?   ¿*Se reconcilian* o *se divorcian*?
¿Quién *es* el padre del niño?   ¿*Gana* las elecciones?   ¿*Ha* usado drogas durante su carrera?

MODELO   Una estrella famosa ha sido arrestada. **¿Qué habrá hecho?**

1. Una estrella famosa está embarazada.

_____

2. Hay rumores de ruptura entre Ana Lago y Javier Paz.

_____

3. Un artista se presentará para gobernador. _____

4. Un deportista ha sido acusado de dopaje. _____

5. Lola Gil y Nacho Sanz han salido besándose en los Premios Onda.

_____

11-33 ¿Será cierto? Two roommates are talking about a possible romance of a famous singer and her co-star in a very popular soap opera. Complete their conversation with the future form of the verbs in parentheses.

— He oído que la cantante Berta Nelson ha terminado su relación con el actor Bernardo Colón.

¿(1) _____ (ser) cierto?

— No sé. ¿(2) _____ (Estar) teniendo Berta un romance con su coprotagonista de *Amores Frustrados*?

— Eso parece. ¿(3) _____ (Divorciarse) de Bernardo? Hacían tan buena pareja...

— Sí, qué lástima. ¿Sabes si Berta (4) _____ (grabar) más episodios para el

próximo año o este escándalo (5) _____ (reducir) el éxito de su telenovela?

— No lo creo. Los periodistas (6) _____ (estar) esperando ver la ruptura de la pareja para promocionar la telenovela más. Ya sabes cómo es el mundo de la farándula.

— ¿(7) _____ (Haber) fotos comprometedoras de Berta y su coprotagonista?

— Es posible, pero no las (8) _____ (publicar) hasta que no tengan más detalles del romance.

— ¿Por qué nos (9) _____ (gustar) tanto lo que pasa en las vidas de los famosos?

— No sé. ¿(10) _____ (Tener, nosotras) los chismes como escape de la vida real?

— No creo. (11) _____ (Llegar) el momento en que nosotras seamos las famosas. No te preocupes.

— Sí, entonces ¿(12) _____ (ser, nosotras) el objetivo de los chismes?

— Claro, así es el mundo de la farándula.

11-34 ¿Qué estarán haciendo? Form sentences using the future progressive tense of the verbs in parentheses to suggest possible explanations for the situations.

MODELO   El futbolista Sancho Lema está con los periodistas. (negar las acusaciones de dopaje)
        Estará negando las acusaciones de dopaje.

1. Los estudiantes están enfrente de la casa del presidente de la universidad. (protestar contra el aumento del precio de la matrícula)

_____

2. El presidente está en la Casa Blanca. (responder a llamadas telefónicas de otros líderes internacionales)

_____

3. Tres policías están en la casa del cantante Pío Ramírez. (arrestarlo por actividades ilegales)

_____

4. La pareja de famosos está en las cortes. (divorciarse legalmente)

_____

5. La cantante Manolita Lunares está entrando en el hospital. (esperar la llegada de su bebé)

_____

6. El actor Rico Pérez y su coprotagonista están besándose en la calle. (grabar episodios de la nueva temporada de *Tormento de Amor*)

_____

11-35 Diario. Are you interested in what celebrities do? Do you follow news about singers, actors and actresses, or professional athletes? Write a paragraph describing two or three celebrities that you find interesting and explain why. Also imagine some unknown things about them that you think are probably true, or make some predictions about the future of each one.

_____

_____

_____

_____

_____

_____

_____

_____

_____

_____

¡A escuchar!

11-36 Todo es mentira. Listen to the story that a reporter from *La Farándula* gives about a possible romance between two co-stars in a popular soap opera. Complete the report with the words that you hear.

Hace días se publicaron fotos muy (1) _____ de los protagonistas de la

telenovela *Rafaela,* Suny Mañas y Santiago Puertas, en la (2) _____ del corazón.

Suny (3) _____ que todo es (4) _____ y que las fotos

son falsas. Suny está (5) _____ y ella y su esposo Tino Vega

(6) _____ un (7) _____ para septiembre. Estas fotos

pueden causar una (8) _____ en la (9) _____ de Suny

y Tino. Suny se niega (*refuses*) a grabar más episodios de la telenovela hasta que las

(10) _____ sean retiradas. La audiencia tendrá que

(11) _____ unas semanas más para ver su (12) _____

favorita, *Rafaela.*

11-37 Suposiciones. Listen to the questions on the recording and say what these people might be doing in the following situations by selecting the logical response from the list and putting the verb in the progressive future. Then as you hear the correct response, write it in the corresponding blank.

anunciar su boda
grabar una película
recibir un premio
grabar una entrevista
proteger la seguridad del partido
establecer relaciones con el líder del país

MODELO   You hear: ¿Qué estará haciendo la policía en el estadio de los Yankees?
You say: **Estará protegiendo la seguridad del partido.**
You hear: Estará protegiendo la seguridad del partido.
You write: **Estará protegiendo la seguridad del partido.**

1. _____

2. _____

3. _____

4. _____

5. _____

¡Trato hecho!

11-38 En la red. Search the Web for two or three Hispanic television networks from around the world. Begin by searching for *cadenas de televisión en español*, or you can also access directly the following Websites: univision.com, telemundo.com, tvazteca.com.mx, rtve.es, tvchile.cl, tvcolombia.com. Check the sites you find for the information requested below and answer the questions in English. Write down the addresses of the interesting and useful sites you discover and share them with your instructor and other students.

Addresses of useful and interesting sites:

www._____

www._____

www._____

1. Compare each network and explain how much information there is about news, sports, soap operas, variety shows, talk shows, documentaries, and shows for children.

   _____

   _____

   _____

   _____

   _____

2. Explain which network you would prefer to watch and why, naming one or two shows you find interesting.

   _____

   _____

   _____

   _____

   _____

   _____

11-39 Composición. Where do you get your news, from TV, from the newspaper, or from the Internet? Which stations, periodicals, or websites do you like in particular? What are the most common topics you see discussed on the news? Which interest or concern you? Do you think that you get a complete, balanced presentation of the news on TV? Do you believe everything that you see on the news? Are there any topics that you think they should talk about more on television? Is there anything that you see too much? Write a paragraph answering these questions. You may incorporate and expand on what you wrote in your **Diarios,** as appropriate.

_____

_____

_____

_____

_____

_____

_____

_____

_____

_____

_____

_____

_____

_____

_____

12   En el extranjero

Tema 1 ¿Qué les dijeron?

12-1 Preparativos. Lucía is going to spend a summer studying political science in Mexico, and since she is very organized, she prepared a checklist with all she has to do before leaving. Complete her list with the appropriate words from those given.

alojamiento	plan de estudios	matricularme	tarjeta de identificación
	matrícula programa asesor solicitar		

☐ 1) _____ mi visa
en el Consulado de México

☐ 2) pagar la _____
antes del 30 de mayo

☐ 3) hablar con mi _____
el miércoles próximo

☐ 4) ir a la página web del _____
de Ciencias Políticas

☐ 5) revisar el _____
de los cursos de verano

☐ 6) encontrar _____
en la universidad en México

☐ 7) enviar la información para obtener mi _____
_____

☐ 8) _____ en los cursos del
otoño antes de salir para México

12-2 No, todavía no. Your friend Ángel is going abroad, but he doesn't seem to be getting everything ready to go. Read the answers that he gives you and come up with the appropriate question in each case, selecting one of the nouns from the list that would elicit the direct object used in the answer.

el pasaporte	la admisión	los pasos a seguir para ser admitido	la matrícula
	las clases el alojamiento la tarjeta de identificación		

MODELO   — ¿Escogiste ya las clases?
            — No, todavía no las escogí.

1. — _____

— No, todavía no la pagué.

2. — _____

— No, todavía no la obtuve.

3. — _____

— No, todavía no lo renové.

4. — _____

— No, todavía no lo encontré.

5. — _____

— No, todavía no la solicité.

6. — _____

— No, todavía no los revisé.

12-3 ¿Ya tienes todo? Gema is asking her sister Belén if she has finished the application process for her semester abroad in Costa Rica. Complete their conversation with the personal pronoun that is appropriate in each case.

— Belén, ¿llamaste a tu asesor para hablar del programa de estudios en el extranjero?

— Sí, (1) _____ llamé, pero su secretaria me dijo que no estaba. Ella (2) _____ dio el teléfono celular de mi asesor.

— Debes hablar con (3) _____ cuanto antes (*as soon as possible*). Recuerda que no puedes matricular_____ (4) si (5) _____ no te aprueba los cursos.

— Sí, ya (6) _____ sé. Pero tengo tantas cosas que hacer...

— A ver, ¿qué más? ¿Ya reservaste el alojamiento?

— Sí, (7) _____ reservé la semana pasada por Internet y tengo una copia de la reserva.

— ¿Dónde (8) _____ tienes? ¿Puedo ver_____ (9)?

— Claro, mira, aquí está, con las fechas y el tipo de habitación. Ahora necesito ir al consulado para solicitar mi visa.

— Sí, ¿sabes cómo hacer_____ (10)?

— Sí, tengo todos los documentos que necesito; sólo tengo que presentar_____ (11) en el consulado y esperar una semana.

— ¿Conoces a los estudiantes que van contigo de tu universidad?

— No (12) _____ conozco a todos, pero conozco a una chica que está en mi clase de historia.

— ¿Cómo (13) _____ llama? ¿(14) _____ conozco (15) _____?

— No, no creo. Se llama Úrsula. (16) _____ viviremos juntas en San José.

— ¡Excelente! Bueno, vamos al consulado antes de que cierren.

12-4 Fui admitido en... Do you remember when you started applying to universities? What were the steps that you had to follow? Answer in Spanish the following questions a friend who is applying to universities might ask, paying special attention to the use of the pronouns and the vocabulary from this **Tema**.

1. ¿Qué pasos tuviste que seguir para solicitar el ingreso a esta universidad?

   _____

   _____

2. ¿Quién te ayudó a solicitar el ingreso en esta universidad? ¿Qué otras universidades te interesaban?

   _____

   _____

3. ¿Fuiste admitido/a en otras universidades? ¿Por qué decidiste asistir a esta universidad?

   _____

   _____

4. ¿Conocías a alguno de tus compañeros/as de clase o de cuarto? ¿Cómo se conocieron tu mejor amigo/a

   de la universidad y tú? _____

   _____

12-5 Diario. Write a paragraph imagining plans to study abroad for the summer, a semester, or a year. What will the advantages and disadvantages be of studying abroad versus staying here? Where are two or three places you would like to go? What are the advantages and disadvantages of each place? Where do you prefer to be housed and why? What are your expectations and what will you need to do to prepare? If you have already studied abroad, you may describe that experience in the past instead.

_____

_____

_____

_____

_____

_____

_____

¡A escuchar!

12-6 Con la asesora. Listen and complete the following conversation between a student and her advisor about next semester, which she is going to spend abroad.

— Buenos días, Estela, ¿en que (1) _____ puedo (2) _____?

— Hola, Profesora Lasarte, voy a estudiar en España el semestre próximo. ¿Podría ayudar_____ (3) con la

selección del (4) _____?

— Por supuesto. ¿Cuándo es la (5) _____ para enviar la (6) _____?

— Debo enviar_____ (7) antes del primero de diciembre. Ya he consultado los distintos

(8) _____ en Internet, y ahora necesito (9) _____ las clases.

— Muy bien, vamos a revisar_____ (10) juntas. ¿Qué clases (11) _____ interesan especialmente?

— Bueno, el curso de Arte Mozárabe, y el de Literatura Contemporánea. También quiero

(12) _____ en (13) _____ cursos especiales, pero no sé cuáles se ofrecen.

— Si escribes un correo electrónico al programa (14) _____

podrán explicar_____ (15) los cursos especiales que ofrecerán en la primavera.

12-7 Cuántas preguntas. Listen to questions a friend is asking you about preparations to study abroad. Answer affirmatively with verbs in the preterite, or negatively with verbs in the present perfect, including the appropriate object or reflexive pronouns. You will then hear the correct response. Listen and write the missing words in the blanks.

MODELO You see: Sí, ya _____. *or* No, todavía no _____.
You hear: ¿Ya entregaste la solicitud en la oficina de estudios en el extranjero?
You say: **Sí, ya la entregué.** *or* **No, todavía no la he entregado.**
You hear: Sí, ya la entregué. *or* No, todavía no la he entregado.
You write: Sí, ya **la entregué**. *or* No, todavía no **la he entregado.**

1. Sí, ya _____.

2. Sí, ya _____.

3. Sí, ya _____.

4. No, todavía no _____.

5. No, todavía no _____.

6. Sí, ya _____.

7. Sí, ya _____.

Tema 2 ¿Podría Ud...? ¿Debería...? ¿Le importaría a Ud.?

12-8 ¿Me podría...? You are meeting with the study abroad representative because you are interested in studying abroad, but you don't know what to do. Use the structure **¿Podría Ud...?** to ask if he/she would help you in the following ways.

1. *provide you information about the program abroad*

   _____

2. *advise you about the plan of studies*

   _____

3. *confirm for you the mandatory subjects in the program*

   _____

4. *tell you the optional subjects in the program*

   _____

5. *explain the steps to follow to be admitted*

   _____

6. *give you a form to apply for the visa*

   _____

12-9 ¿Qué deberían...? Use **debería** with the indicated verbs to say which documents from the list below people should present, obtain, or apply for in the following situations. Use at least two different verbs with different documents for each situation.

presentar	un acta de nacimiento
obtener	el certificado de secundaria
solicitar	un pasaporte vigente
	una carta de solvencia del banco
	una visa
	un impreso de admisión en el programa

1. Un estudiante que va a pasar un semestre estudiando en el extranjero.

   _____

   _____

2. Una persona que quiere abrir un negocio en un país extranjero.

   _____

   _____

3. Los estudiantes que están solicitando el ingreso a la universidad.

   _____

   _____

12-10 Sería perfecto... Diana is studying in Barcelona and she writes her friend Alberto to tell him how things are going. Complete her letter with the conditional tense of the verbs in parentheses.

Querido Alberto,

Hace dos días que llegué a Barcelona y como te prometí que te (1)_____ (escribir), aquí va mi carta. Barcelona es una ciudad moderna, con muchos lugares interesantes. Estoy segura de que te (2)_____ (encantar); además tú hablas español muy bien y (3)_____ (poder) practicarlo con tantas chicas guapas que hay en la ciudad. Me gusta mucho la familia con quien vivo, comparto el cuarto con una chica francesa, Monique. Me gusta Monique, pero (4)_____ (preferir) tener una habitación para mí sola. Las clases son muy entretenidas; nuestra profesora de arte nos prometió que (5)_____ (ir) a visitar el Templo de la Sagrada Familia la próxima semana. No puedo esperar. Pensaba que (6)_____ (ser) muy difícil adaptarme a las costumbres (customs) del país, pero no estoy teniendo problemas. La comida es fantástica; muchos estudiantes me dijeron que me (7)_____ (gustar) mucho la comida de España y tenían razón. Alberto, (8)_____ (deber) visitarme, lo (9)_____ (pasar, nosotros) muy bien. (10)_____ (viajar, nosotros) a la Costa Brava, te (11)_____ (mostrar) los museos de Picasso, Dalí y Miró, y (12)_____ (probar, nosotros) los mejores restaurantes de Barcelona.

Ya sé que la boda de tu hermana es el quince de junio, pero (13)_____ (pasar) diez días conmigo después de que las clases terminen, y (14)_____ (volver) a tiempo para la boda.

Piénsalo, te extraño mucho,

Diana

12-11 ¿Qué dijeron? A friend was not listening to instructions. Repeat the information that the following people give by using the conditional of the verb that originally appears in future.

MODELO "Primero deberán rellenar un formulario con información personal."
La secretaría nos dijo que **primero deberíamos rellenar un formulario con información personal.**

1. "La fecha límite de matrícula terminará el primero de mayo para los estudiantes de nuevo ingreso."

   El director de la oficina de estudios en el extranjero dijo que _____

   _____.

2. "Los estudiantes extranjeros tendrán que presentar una fotocopia del pasaporte vigente."

   El asesor nos informó que _____

   _____.

3. "Sólo trece estudiantes recibirán ayuda económica para estudiar en el extranjero."

   El presidente de la universidad dijo que _____

   _____.

4. "El Cónsul legalizará el acta de nacimiento original sin ningún problema."

   El secretario nos dijo que _____

   _____.

5. "Les asesoraré sobre las asignaturas obligatorias y optativas que ofrece el programa."

   Nuestro profesor nos prometió que _____

   _____.

12-12 Diario. Is the situation in your university ideal? What aspects of your school would you change? Are there enough resources for students? Is the library modern and well-equipped? Are the facilities up-to-date? Are there enough scholarships, classes, parking...? Write a paragraph in the conditional tense explaining how things would be ideally.

_____

_____

_____

_____

_____

_____

¡A escuchar!

12-13 Hola, buenas tardes. Listen to a conversation between a student and an assistant from the study abroad program. Fill in the blanks with the missing words that you hear.

— Hola, buenas tardes, ¿en qué (1) _____ atenderlo?

— Buenas tardes, quisiera saber los documentos que (2) _____ obtener para solicitar la admisión a su programa.

— Si es usted estudiante extranjero, necesita presentar una fotocopia del pasaporte

(3) _____, un (4) _____, y el

(5) _____ de solicitud de admisión.

— El acta de nacimiento, ¿debe estar (6) _____ por el Cónsul?

— Sí, así es, y debe ser un documento (7) _____.

— ¿Y le (8) _____ decirme adónde debo (9) _____ la documentación?

— Por supuesto. Debe enviar la documentación en un (10) _____ a la oficina de

(11) _____ y (12) _____.
— Muchas gracias por su ayuda.

— Ha sido un placer.

12-14 Un sistema perfecto. Listen to the following statements and change the verbs to the conditional to describe an ideal university. Then repeat as you hear the answer, and fill in the missing words.

MODELO	You see:	Todos los estudiantes _____.
	You hear:	Todos los estudiantes estudian una lengua extranjera.
	You say:	**Todos los estudiantes estudiarían una lengua extranjera.**
	You hear:	Todos los estudiantes estudiarían una lengua extranjera.
	You repeat:	**Todos los estudiantes estudiarían una lengua extranjera.**
	You write:	Todos los estudiantes **estudiarían una lengua extranjera.**

1. Los estudios universitarios _____ gratuitos (*free*) para todos los estudiantes.

2. Todos los estudiantes _____ estudiando en el extranjero.

3. Los estudiantes _____ todos los recursos que necesitan.

4. Todos los profesores _____ dispuestos (*ready, willing*) a ayudar a los estudiantes.

5. Las clases _____ y todos _____.

6. Las instalaciones deportivas _____ y accesibles para todos los estudiantes.

Tema 3 ¿Es necesario?

12-15 Nacionalidades. Read the information about these famous Hispanics and write sentences giving their nationalities.

MODELO   Mario Vargas Llosa es un escritor famoso que ganó el Premio Nóbel de Literatura. Nació en Arequipa, una ciudad al sur de Lima.
Mario Vargas Llosa es peruano.

1. Frida Kahlo y Diego Rivera fueron pintores famosos nacidos en Coyoacán y Guanajuato, respectivamente.

   _____

2. Eva Perón fue un gran personaje en la escena política y nació en Buenos Aires.

   _____

3. Gabriel García Márquez es un escritor muy conocido por obras como *Cien años de soledad*. Nació en Aracataca, al norte de Bogotá.

   _____

4. Gloria Estefan nació en La Habana y emigró a Estados Unidos, a Miami, a la edad de dos años.

   _____

5. Julia Álvarez es una novelista nacida en Nueva York que emigró a la República Dominicana cuando era niña. Sus obras reflejan sus raíces dominicanas.

   _____

6. Pedro Almodóvar es un conocido director de cine que nació en Ciudad Real, una provincia al sur de Madrid. Ha dirigido películas tan famosas como *Mujeres al borde de un ataque de nervios* y *Hable con ella*.

   _____

Now complete the following statements about one of the people listed above. Fill in the first blank with the conditional of the verb in parentheses and complete the other blanks with your own opinion.

a. Me _____ (gustar) conocer a _____

   porque _____.

b. _____ (hablar, yo) con él/ella de _____

   _____.

c. Le _____ (preguntar, yo) _____

   _____.

12-16 Se necesitan... Read the following job posting for government employees in the Immigration and Naturalization Department. Complete the advertisement with the appropriate verbs from the list in the subjunctive.

proporcionar	entender	tramitar	revisar	tener	atender

Se necesitan funcionarios de inmigración que

(1) _____ a la gente con amabilidad, que

(2) _____ información sobre la obtención de

visas y pasaportes, que (3) _____ las solicitudes

de ciudadanía y residencia permanente y que (4) _____ las peticiones de

renovación de visa. Se buscan personas que (5) _____ las leyes de inmigración y

que (6) _____ la nacionalidad estadounidense.

12-17 Tramitar la visa. The study abroad counselor is advising students who are getting ready to spend a semester in a foreign university. Does she recommend doing or not doing the following things? Write sentences in the subjunctive, as in the **modelo.**

MODELO   más vale que / (no) esperar mucho para buscar alojamiento
Más vale que no esperen mucho para buscar alojamiento.

1. es importante que / (no) tramitar la visa en el último momento en el consulado o la embajada

   _____

2. más vale que / (no) sacar fotos tamaño pasaporte antes de ir al consulado o la embajada

   _____

3. es necesario que / (no) presentar un estado de su cuenta personal o de la cuenta de sus padres

   _____

4. les recomiendo que / (no) rellenar la solicitud de visa con cuidado

   _____

5. es necesario que / (no) renovar la visa en caso de permanecer en el país

   _____

6. es importante que / (no) ser impacientes

   _____

12-18 Con tal de que... Link the following sentences using the logical conjunction in parentheses. Put the main verb in the future form for **tú,** unless another subject is indicated, and put the verb after the conjunction in the subjunctive.

MODELO necesitar presentar una carta de solvencia (con tal que / a menos que) tener una beca
Necesitarás presentar una carta de solvencia a menos que tengas una beca.

1. poder permanecer en el país (a menos que / con tal que) renovar la visa

   _____

2. no escoger el programa de estudios (para que / hasta que) no hablar con tu asesor

   _____

3. no obtener una tarjeta de identificación (para que / a menos que) presentarse en sus oficinas

   _____

4. poder estudiar en el extranjero (con tal que / a menos que) entregar la solicitud antes de la fecha límite

   _____

5. deber tramitar una visa (con tal que / a menos que) ser ciudadano del país

   _____

6. el acta de nacimiento no ser válida (a menos que / para que) estar legalizada por el Cónsul

   _____

12-19 Diario. Did you ever travel to another country? Describe your trip. How long were you there? Did you have to obtain a passport? Where did you go to get it? Was it difficult to complete the application? When you arrived in the foreign country, did you have a visa? Did you have to fill out a tourist visa application? What kind of information did you have to provide? If you've never traveled to another country, talk about an experience traveling in the United States. How has the situation in the airports changed in recent years? Did you ever witness an unpleasant situation in an airport? Describe it.

_____

_____

_____

_____

_____

_____

¡A escuchar!

12-20 ¿Hay alguien que...? Martina works at the Immigration Office in Miami, and her friend Ana is asking her questions. Write down the missing parts of Ana's questions, then imagine how Martina responds and complete her answers.

MODELO   You see: — ¿Hay alguien que _____ en las oficinas siempre?

                            — Sí, un funcionario _____ siempre.

            You hear: ¿Hay alguien que me pueda atender en las oficinas siempre?

            You write: — ¿Hay alguien que **me pueda atender** en las oficinas siempre?

                            — Sí, un funcionario **te puede atender** siempre.

1. — ¿Hay funcionarios de inmigración que _____?

    — Sí, hay muchos funcionarios de inmigración que _____.

2. — ¿Hay países que _____ consulado cerca de Miami?

    — Sí, hay varios países que _____ consulado cerca de Miami.

3. — ¿Hay consulados que _____?

    — No, todos los consulados _____.

4. — ¿Hay pasaportes que _____?

    — No, todos los pasaportes _____.

5. — ¿Hay muchos inmigrantes que _____?

    — Sí, hay muchos inmigrantes que _____.

12-21 Dudo que... Express doubts about the occurrence of what is mentioned in the statements or questions you hear. You will then hear the correct answer. Listen and repeat, and fill in the missing words in the blanks.

MODELO   You see: Dudo que _____ la visa.

            You hear: Te darán la visa, no te preocupes.

            You say: **Dudo que me den la visa.**

            You hear: Dudo que me den la visa.

            You repeat: **Dudo que me den la visa.**

            You write: Dudo que **me den** la visa.

1. Dudo que _____ en el país por varios meses.

2. Dudo que _____ mi visa por tener un buen trabajo.

3. Dudo que _____ la residencia permanente el próximo año.

4. Dudo que _____ ciudadano americano en el 2011.

5. Dudo que _____ votar en las próximas elecciones presidenciales.

Tema 4 ¿Qué le dijeron que hiciera?

12-22 En la Oficina de Inmigración. Soledad needs to apply for a visa. Look at the illustrations below and write sentences explaining what she did in order to handle the paperwork. Use the expressions from the list and conjugate the verbs in the preterite.

entregar los documentos	completar los formularios	hacer una cita por teléfono
hablar con el funcionario	hacer cola	acudir a la hora prevista	esperar su turno

1.

2.

3.

4.

5.

6.

1. _____

2. _____

3. _____

4. _____

5. _____

6. _____

12-23 ¡Vaya día! Complete the following conversations between a mother and her daughter, who is talking about her tedious day at the Immigration Office. Use the expressions from the list.

esperar	papeleo	visa	funcionarios	prevista
acudir	domicilio	hacer cola	cita	tarifas

— Hola, mamá. Ya estoy de vuelta.

— Hola, hija. ¿Cómo te fue con el (1) _____?

— Bueno, ahora ya está terminado, pero fue muy pesado (*tedious, a hassle*). Había muchísima gente en la

oficina y tuve que (2) _____ mi turno por tres horas.

— Oh, no. ¿Hiciste una (3) _____ por teléfono antes de ir?

— Sí, y fui a la oficina a la hora (4) _____, pero tuve que

(5) _____ igualmente. Después, se me olvidó en el coche el documento que

mostraba nuestro (6) _____. Así que tuve que volver al coche por un recibo

de la luz y (7) _____ de nuevo a las oficinas.

— ¿En serio? ¿Te atendieron bien los (8) _____?

— Sí, la señora era muy amable. Fue culpa mía (*my fault*) por no tener todos los documentos. Pero ahora

ya se ha terminado el proceso, ya pagué mis (9) _____ y en dos semanas

recibiré mi (10) _____.

12-24 Entonces, ¿qué pasó? Eduardo couldn't turn in his visa application because he was missing a document. Complete the following sentences with the logical endings from the list, conjugating the infinitives in the imperfect subjunctive.

volver mañana con la documentación decirme los documentos darme una cita
necesitar un comprobante de domicilio tramitar correctamente mi visa mostrar mi domicilio

1. Primero, llamé por teléfono para que el funcionario _____.

2. También le pedí que _____ requeridos para obtener una visa.

3. No tenía un documento que _____.

4. No creía que la oficina _____.

5. El funcionario quería que _____ completa.

6. Me importaba que la oficina _____.

12-25 ¿Qué les dijo? Did the study abroad office representative tell foreign students to do or not to do the following things? Complete the sentences as in the **modelo.**

MODELO   El representante les dijo que **no escogieran los cursos sin la ayuda de su consejero.**
                    (escoger los cursos sin la ayuda de su consejero)

1. El representante les dijo que _____.
   (estar preparados para el comienzo del curso)

2. El representante les dijo que _____.
   (acudir a la reunión de información para estudiantes extranjeros)

3. El representante les dijo que _____.
   (presentarse en la oficina para obtener una tarjeta de identificación)

4. El representante les dijo que _____.
   (matricularse para las clases del otoño)

5. El representante les dijo que _____.
   (realizar el papeleo en el último momento)

6. El representante les dijo que _____.
   (pagar las tarifas de matrícula después de la fecha límite)

12-26 Diario. What advice did your parents give you before you started at the university? What did they tell you to do or not to do? Who else gave you advice? What did they advise you to do or not to do? Use the preterite of verbs like **decir, recomendar, aconsejar,** or **prohibir** followed by the imperfect subjunctive to say what they told you (not) to do.

_____

_____

_____

_____

_____

_____

_____

_____

_____

_____

¡A escuchar!

12-27 Un servicio valioso. Listen to the following information about the valuable services that the immigration and naturalization offices provide to citizens and residents of a country. Complete the text with the words that you hear.

Cada día las oficinas de (1) _____ abren sus puertas a miles de individuos que

(2) _____ a este lugar para (3) _____ sus trámites

para (4) _____ su visa y (5) _____ en el país,

(6) _____ la ciudadanía, o simplemente obtener un

(7) _____. Las personas generalmente (8) _____

pacientemente para hablar con los (9) _____, entregar los

(10) _____ y pagar las (11) _____. La Oficina de

Inmigración (12) _____ servicios muy valiosos a los

(13) _____ y a los (14) _____ del país.

12-28 Expectativas diferentes. You are going to hear a conversation between two students, Quique and Olga, talking about what they wanted in a university before they started school. First, pause the recording and write the imperfect subjunctive of the infinitives in parentheses. Then turn on the recording, listen to the conversation, and indicate whether each sentence describes Quique's or Olga's preference by placing an **X** in the correct blank.

MODELO   You write: Quería que la universidad **tuviera** (tener) un campus bonito.
              You listen and indicate: _____ Quique _**X**_ Olga

1. _____ Quique _____ Olga: Quería que la universidad _____ (tener) diversidad de estudiantes.

2. _____ Quique _____ Olga: Quería que la biblioteca _____ (ser) buena.

3. _____ Quique _____ Olga: Quería que la universidad _____ (atender) bien a los estudiantes.

4. _____ Quique _____ Olga: Quería que la universidad _____ (proporcionar) recursos tecnológicos.

5. _____ Quique _____ Olga: Quería que los profesores _____ (asesorar) a los estudiantes.

6. _____ Quique _____ Olga: Quería que los estudiantes y profesores _____ (realizar) trabajo comunitario.

7. _____ Quique _____ Olga: Quería que la universidad _____ (dar) becas por jugar deportes.

8. _____ Quique _____ Olga: Quería que _____ (haber) un buen programa en el extranjero.

Tema 5 Les agradecería...

12-29 Estimados señores. Complete the following letter that Leticia wrote to the **Universidad de las Américas** in Puebla requesting information about their programs for foreign students with the appropriate expressions from the list.

solicitar	agradecería	a la espera de	fechas límite	tarifas	confirmar	acerca de
quisiera	alojamiento	con referencia	dirijo	atentamente	obtener	estimados

Leticia Santiago
10 Broad Street
Providence, RI 02906

28 de noviembre, 2004

Universidad de las Américas
Programas Internacionales
Sta. Catarina Mártir
Cholula, Puebla
C.P. 72820. México

(1)_____ señores:

Me (2)_____ a ustedes con la intención de

(3)_____ información sobre los Programas

Internacionales de la Universidad de las Américas en Puebla.

(4)_____ saber más sobre la oferta académica de

su programa y sobre las (5)_____ de

matrícula. Les (6)_____ me

enviarían más información (7)_____ los cursos de

primavera en particular.

Deseo (8)_____ también que ofrecen

(9)_____ para los estudiantes extranjeros en familias de la

ciudad y que los precios de las (10)_____ son las

que aparecen en su página web. (11)_____

_____ al trámite de la visa, necesitaría saber el tipo de

documento que necesito (12)_____ en el consulado.

(13)_____ su respuesta, se despide

(14)_____,

Leticia Santiago
Leticia Santiago

12-30 Soluciones para Arancha. Arancha has a very pessimistic attitude and never thinks that problems have a solution. Say what you would do in these situations, using the phrases in parentheses.

MODELO   No puedo hablar con mi asesor porque no tengo su teléfono.
(enviarle un correo electrónico)
Si no pudiera hablar con mi asesor porque no tengo su teléfono, le enviaría un correo electrónico.

1. No puedo estudiar en el extranjero sin perder mi beca.
   (escoger un programa de voluntariado en el extranjero durante el verano)

   _____

2. No puedo permanecer en el país porque mi visa no está vigente.
   (prolongar la visa en el consulado)

   _____

3. No puedo tramitar mi solicitud de residencia hoy porque hay una cola tremenda.
   (tramitar la solicitud por Internet)

   _____

4. No puedo hablar con mi asesor en sus horas de oficina.
   (tratar de hacer una cita a otra hora)

   _____

5. No puedo hacer amistades fácilmente porque soy muy tímida.
   (participar en más actividades sociales de la universidad)

   _____

12-31 Hipótesis. Complete the following conversation between two friends with the verbs in parentheses in the conditional or imperfect subjunctive, as appropriate.

— Darío, ¿cómo estás? Pareces preocupado.

— Sí, no estoy muy bien hoy. Envié la solicitud de ingreso al programa de Salamanca y no he sido

admitido. ¿Cómo estarías tú si (1) _____ (recibir) tan malas noticias?

— Pues igual que tú. Si no fuera admitida en el programa de Santiago, me (2) _____ (enojar) mucho.

— El problema son mis notas. Si (3) _____ (probar) que mis notas son mejores, podría tener una oportunidad.

— Puedes intentarlo de nuevo (*attempt it again*), ¿no? Si (4) _____ (querer), sacarías notas muy altas en tus clases. Eres muy inteligente, pero también muy perezoso.

— Sí, ya lo sé. Si me presentara a todas las clases y (5) _____ (entregar) todas las tareas a tiempo, no tendría notas tan bajas.

— Es una buena lección.

— Cecilia, si tú me ayudaras a tener disciplina te lo (6) _____ (agradecer) mucho.

— Por supuesto. Desde el lunes nos encontraremos en la biblioteca todas las tardes a las seis.

12-32 Si pudiera... Answer the following questions a classmate might ask you with complete sentences in Spanish.

1. Si pudieras escoger cualquier universidad del país, ¿a cuál asistirías? ¿Por qué?

   _____

   _____

2. Si no tuvieras que tomar asignaturas obligatorias, ¿qué tipo de asignaturas tomarías? ¿Por qué?

   _____

   _____

3. Si pudieras cambiar cualquier aspecto de tu vida en la universidad, ¿qué cambiarías?

   _____

   _____

12-33 Diario. If you could spend a semester abroad, which country would you choose? Why? What do you know about the country that makes it so interesting? If you could choose any classes to take abroad, which ones would you select? Why?

_____

_____

_____

_____

_____

_____

_____

_____

_____

_____

_____

¡A escuchar!

12-34 En respuesta a su carta. Listen to the response that the **Universidad de las Américas** in Puebla gives Leticia regarding her request for information on the international programs, and complete the letter with the words that you hear.

Universidad de las Américas. Programas Internacionales
Sta. Catarina Mártir Cholula, Puebla
C.P. 72820. México

8 de diciembre, 2004

Leticia Santiago
10 Broad Street
Providence, RI 02906

(1)_____ Leticia:

(2)_____ a su carta del pasado 28 de noviembre,

(3)_____ agradecerle su interés en nuestros Programas

Internacionales. (4)_____ le envío la información actualizada

de los cursos de primavera y las tarifas de alojamiento que nos solicitó. Tenemos

(5)_____ ofrecer cursos adicionales a los que aparecen en el

catálogo, pero todavía no tenemos esa información. Para (6)_____

su visa, le aconsejo que (7)_____ al Consulado de México en

Boston, y allí la (8)_____. Esperamos tenerla con nosotros

el próximo curso.

(9)_____,

Ángeles Calzada
Ángeles Calzada

12-35 ¿Cómo reaccionarías? Listen to the following situations and react according to the cues. You will then hear the correct answer. Repeat, pause the recording, and write the answer in the space provided.

MODELO   You see: enojarse:
                 You hear: Si mi profesor no respondiera a mis llamadas...
                 You say: **Si mi profesor no respondiera a mis llamadas, me enojaría.**
                 You hear: Si mi profesor no respondiera a mis llamadas, me enojaría.
                 You repeat: **Si mi profesor no respondiera a mis llamadas, me enojaría.**
                 You write: <u>**Si mi profesor no respondiera a mis llamadas, me enojaría.**</u>

1. no hacer nada: _____

2. quejarse: _____

3. agradecérselo: _____

4. enojarse: _____

¡Trato hecho!

12-36 En la red. Search the Web for the preferred study abroad destinations for students learning Spanish as a foreign language. Begin by searching for *learn Spanish abroad*. Check the sites you find for the information requested below and answer the questions in English. Write down the addresses of the interesting and useful sites you discover and share them with your instructor and other students.

Addresses of useful and interesting sites:

www._____

www._____

www._____

1. What are three of the most popular study abroad options for studying Spanish? What are some of the recommendations provided to students who wish to go abroad?

   _____

   _____

   _____

2. What are some of the objectives of the Language Immersion programs? Why are Immersion Programs so effective?

   _____

   _____

   _____

3. What are some of the advantages of the Volunteer Programs in foreign countries? Would you choose this kind of program over a more traditional study abroad option? Explain why or why not.

   _____

   _____

   _____

12-37 Composición. Using what you have written in each **Diario** section for this chapter and adding other details, write about your current life and the decisions that you have made so far concerning your education. Are you satisfied with them? What would you change if you could? How would you like your life to be? What type of career (**una carrera**) would you select if you had the opportunity? Would you consider living in another country if it were beneficial for (**beneficioso para**) your career? What benefits (**los beneficios**) would there be in living in another country?

_____

_____

_____

_____

_____

_____

_____

_____

_____

_____

_____

_____

_____

_____

_____

_____

_____

_____

NOTAS

NOTAS

NOTAS

NOTAS

NOTAS

NOTAS

NOTAS

NOTAS

NOTAS

NOTAS

NOTAS

NOTAS

NOTAS

NOTAS

NOTAS

NOTAS

NOTAS

NOTAS

NOTAS

NOTAS